# RUNNING FOR MY LIFE

# RUNNING FOR MY LIFE

On the extreme road with adventure runner Ray Zahab

## Ray Zahab

INSOMNIAC PRESS

For my brother, John.

# Acknowledgments

There are so many people to whom I'd like to express my gratitude. I really need to thank my bro, John. He is my inspiration—and if I didn't follow him into the great outdoors, I would never have realized my dreams. I am so grateful for my incredible wife, Kathy: I am lucky to have my best friend and soulmate on this crazy journey. You keep me both buoyant and grounded, and I love you. Mom and Dad: I thank you for the true gift of choice. You taught us to follow our passion, and to appreciate all that life can give…and take away. Brian Henderson, for running every step of this journey with me. Michael and Gillian Edelson, my alternate family, there's too much to thank you for! Nancy Manning, for teaching me to believe in myself. Brenda Hamm, you gave me the chance to follow a new path. Pat Doyle, for teaching me to run, suffer, and for introducing me to the concept of "ultra." Sasja Nieujkerk, my best friend during some really tough times. Jodi Bigelow, the type of friend who accepts you and does not judge. I am lucky to count myself as one of your friends. Dave Lightfoot, my childhood best friend. Although we've gone on to separate paths, I will never forget the awesome good times we had as kids right through college. Lisa Smith-Batchen, for believing in my dreams and never saying I couldn't do it. I'm forever grateful for the gift of her knowledge. Kevin Lin, my other brother. Charlie Engle, lots of miles together! Greg Christie: He's Mr. Chelsea, and he rocks. Duane Smith, thank you for keeping my legs attached to me and working. Jen Segger, the toughest woman I know. You are true inspiration. Dave McMahon and Lise Meloche: to Dave, thank you for teaching me to run—literally, and Lise…"Pain is temporary".... Karen Nesbitt, for your courage in facing life's ups and downs. The bravest person I know. The Touareg, the soul of the Sahara. Many of you are my friends. Mike at Insomniac Press, for giving me the chance to tell my story. And there are so many more of you. Ken Davidson, Evan Solomon, Shirley Thompson, Scott Smith, Jennifer Taylor, Tony Hatoum, Footie, Greg Lesniewski, Saint, Rob Diniz, Mark Tamminga, Jimmy Winfield, Snowman, Anton Stranc, Jay Smith, Ryan Grant, Marshall Ulrich, Terry Thompson, Kelly-Ann, Ann Scharfe, Christine B…thank you all. You'll never know how much you mean to me.

# Table of Contents

# Prologue
## December 2003

I'm an adventurer runner. That's something that a lot of people know about me. But something that most people don't know about me is that I've got a problem with my spine. It's called spondylolisthesis, and it's a condition that can be more painful to have than it is to pronounce. It means that my back isn't straight. It's as if there are little hairline fractures in my spine, and the scarring in the bone can cause a ton of issues, like spondylosis, which is a swelling of the spinal canal. I won't get into any more detail. Suffice it to say that from the time I was fifteen years old, I've had a lot of pain in my back, hips, and legs. When my doctor first diagnosed me, I'd asked him what I could do about it.

"Physio," he'd told me. "Apart from that, don't go horseback riding, and avoid running. Try to strengthen your back with free weights."

If it weren't for this condition, I wouldn't have been forced to go for regular chiropractor visits, and if it wasn't for one of those visits in particular, I might never have become the runner I am today.

The day that changed my life started out in an ordinary way. I was sitting in the waiting room of my chiropractor's office, a little early for my weekly appointment with Dr. Duane Smith. I was sitting in one of Dr. Smith's big comfortable chairs and listening to a soft-rock station, which was piped in through the radio. Duane's assistant was sitting at her desk, humming along to a song I recognized but couldn't place. I picked up a magazine on the table next to me: a copy of *Explore*. I started to flip through the pages.

The pictures immediately amazed me. Wow, I thought, what a cool magazine! What a cool concept! All the people in those pictures looked so strong and happy—so alive! As I was thumbing through the magazine, I came across a picture that floored me. It was from a race called the Yukon Arctic Ultra.

It was a picture of some dude in the Yukon. He was running with a sled attached to him. It was dark out and you could see the great Northern sky behind him, the stars and the moon. It looked like he was running towards the ends of the earth. It was amazing!

As I began to read the article, I was blown away. The race looked wild. The article went on to talk about some of the details from the previous year's race: the insanely low temperatures, the heavy sleds the racers dragged behind them, the unforgiving terrain. I was in total awe, but those were really just details. What astonished me was the fact that the race was 160 kilometres long, non-stop!

Who does this? I thought.

They've got be crazy, I thought.

And then, before I knew it, I was thinking something like: this looks *so* cool.

Just then, Dr. Smith poked his head out of his office door, signalling to me that he was ready for our appointment. I took one last look at the article before putting the magazine down.

Something in me had clicked. The next race was in just under three months, and I knew that I wasn't going to miss it. Never mind the fact that I'd never run a race before in my life!

That, in a nutshell, was how, at the age of thirty-four, my life changed forever.

# CHAPTER ONE

Childhood
The '70s

I wasn't always someone who believed in myself or sought out adventure: those were qualities I learned.

I grew up in the village of Carp, Ontario, a small farming community west of Ottawa, with my mom and dad and younger brother, John. I had, for all intents and purposes, a great childhood. It was farm life: I was surrounded by family and friends, lots of greenery and trees, and as a kid I spent a great deal of time riding horses, playing with the neighbours, and spending time visiting with my family in Ohio.

Both my parents were professionals. My mom, Nancy, was a nurse, and my father, Raymond, was a surgeon. Although they made a decent living, they both came from humble beginnings, so they knew the importance of hard work. My dad in particular had made great leaps and bounds in his life. He grew up in a tiny village in the mountains of Lebanon, amongst his five brothers and sisters in a house the size of most people's living room. My father's family—like so many other families in Lebanon—wanted to move to Canada. My father had family in Canada, and so he decided to make a go of it here in his late teens. He worked hard, and eventually studied at the University of Ottawa in medical school. He was later invited to do his residency in the United States. The transition from Lebanon to North America must have been a really tough one for him. I have always respected the hard work he put into all aspects of his life, especially with his career as a surgeon.

My mom and dad met while my father was doing his

residency at St. Thomas in Ohio. My mom knew that she wanted to meet him. One day, with a full tray of medicine in her hands, she smashed right into him, dropping the tray and its contents in front of my father. That got his attention all right. How could it not? She was a knockout! She was tall and blond, with pretty hazel eyes. They were married a few years later. They moved to Ottawa, where my father took a job at Grace Hospital. I was born shortly thereafter.

My parents worked hard, and they taught John and me to work hard too. When I was ten years old and John was nine, my mother told us it was time we learned how to take care of ourselves. We learned how to cook, clean, sew, and do the laundry. My mom had a great big wooden spoon that she would bring out when John or I talked back or acted lazy. But I'll tell you something: she never had to use it once! Just the sight of that thing would get our butts in gear.

I loved living in the country. Our closest neighbours were the Bruces, who lived about twenty-five acres across the field from our house. John and I would run over there to splash around in their pool and play with their kids. A couple of kilometres away from our home, we had a barn where we kept horses. I used to run over there in my cowboy boots to feed and tend to them everyday. I pretended I was a cowboy. I loved those horses tremendously. In those days, my brother used to ride with me, although as we got older John got into other sports.

My best friend was a boy named Dave Lightfoot. We managed to get into all kinds of trouble, as little boys do, and some of my happiest memories are of the two of us pedalling our bikes around town or going down to the lake and throwing out our lines. We made our own fun in the country. We built tree houses, perfected the art of stone skipping, played tag or kick the can, and made up our own games with our own rules.

My father was a very busy man, and so it was our mother who raised us on a day-to-day basis. Even as a kid, I knew my father did important work and I respected him for it. Although he was out of the house a lot, his family was very important to him. He always made sure that we had Sunday dinner together, and I distinctly remember the happy feeling I would get when I would watch my dad helping my mom out around the kitchen and when he would sit down at the head of our table and tell us all jokes. My father was full of energy, a fast talker, and a generally happy man. That made all of us happy too.

It was important to my parents that we weren't spoiled, and they were careful to make sure we appreciated what we had. As a kid, one of my favourite things was a 45 record player. It sat in our living room, and I loved that thing almost as much as our horses. I'd sit in front of it for hours on end, my ear plastered to the speaker while I tapped my fingers or toes to the beat of the music.

My favourite music was the stuff that my uncle Tom played for us. He lived in Ohio, in a house near my grandpa and grandma. John and I visited with them every summer. My grandfather took us out fishing, and Uncle Tom took us for rides in his red Jeep. We drove around the country roads with the music blasting. He had an eight-track player in the car—at the time, there was nothing cooler. He introduced us to Neil Young, The Allman Brothers, Johnny Cash, Waylon Jennings, and Willie Nelson. Those were the records we'd beg my mom to buy us when we got home. From the time I was eight years old I loved rock 'n' roll.

One afternoon when I was about nine, my mom came home with a new record for us. I was so excited to put it on that I grabbed it out of her hands and placed the needle on the record immediately. But it wasn't music: instead it was a strange little story about a kid who wouldn't stop asking his parents for things. Eventually, all that whining broke his parents' hearts. When the story was over, I was so sad. I didn't want to do that! The story got me thinking about how lucky I was. After that, I don't think I took the things we had for granted.

Although my parents taught us to work hard and to look after ourselves, they were also lenient with us. John and I didn't have the same restrictions that some of the other kids had. We were allowed to roam the countryside or go for long bike rides unaccompanied. Not to say that we were free to do *whatever* we wanted, but our parents trusted in our good sense. Later on, the same kind of attitude applied in school. My parents didn't demand that we brought home straight A's—in fact, it's fair to say that they truly never put any pressure on us at all. In many ways, I think that was the greatest gift they ever gave us. We were free to be ourselves, no questions asked.

# CHAPTER TWO

High School
The Mid-'80s

The confidence and ease I had as a kid started to wane as I got older. By the time I was ready to go to high school, it had melted away completely. In the weeks leading up to my first day in grade nine, I was panic-stricken. What I was the most scared of was gym class. Of all the things about high school that I found intimidating, phys. ed. had me totally freaked out.

I wasn't athletic in a conventional way. I rode horses, there was *that*, but we weren't going to be riding horses at school! I was active, sure, but so was everyone in the country. The fact was that I couldn't throw a ball to save my life. I couldn't play football, I sucked at baseball, and I was a complete joke when it came to basketball. In my adolescent brain, I thought that, as a guy, those were the things I was *supposed* to be good at.

It might sound trivial, but back then it was a big deal to me. I imagined myself being looked over when it came to dodge ball or football teams, and the humiliation was overwhelming. I *knew* gym class was going to suck.

It did suck. It was everything I had thought it would be and worse. During classes where we had to pick teams, I was almost always the last kid chosen. Standing there in my gym shorts, waiting for someone to call my name, made me feel like the biggest loser in the room. I didn't have the skills to cope with those kinds of feelings at the time. I couldn't escape the feeling that I didn't have any skill, that I wasn't good at anything. It pervaded other parts of my life until the idea became like my own kind of self-inflicted torture.

In grade ten, we did track and field and I ran the 2,400 metre run. Even though I logged a decent time, and placed 4th, the coaches were already too preoccupied with the star jocks to care about me. I never blamed my teachers because I understood that they had a lot on their plates, but being overlooked was the worst. I wanted to wave my arms and shout at them, "Hey! Look over here! I can run too!" but I knew they'd ignore me. It hurt.

Eventually, that feeling of being overlooked permeated every aspect of my life. I stopped thinking of myself as someone with potential and started thinking of myself as someone who simply wasn't good at anything. What I really wanted was someone to pat me on the back and tell me that I was all right. Looking back on it, I had hoped that someone would notice that I was a decent enough runner to want to coach me. When that didn't happened, I figured that it didn't make any difference what I did—no one would notice anyway.

I got to a point where I lost interested in school entirely. I just wanted to get through the week. I didn't prepare for exams or tests, and if a big project came up, I had no idea how I was going to get through it. If I studied at all it was on the bus on the way to school. I didn't even want to try. I figured since I was bound to fail, what was the point?

From a social perspective, however, school was lots of fun. I had great friends. I wasn't one of "the cool kids," but I felt at ease bopping around from one group to another. I was friendly with the jocks, the punk rock kids, with the so-called nerdy kids. Like my father, I was an extrovert and was able to make friends with just about anyone.

The strange thing about it is that while I always *appeared* to be the happy-go-lucky kid, the truth was that underneath it all I was actually incredibly unhappy. Most kids in high school go through periods of depression, but I was *really* unhappy for long periods of time. I never showed it though, and I certainly never talked about it.

I think it was those unhappy feelings, and keeping them so bottled up, that eventually led me down a self-destructive path. Looking back, I wish I had talked to someone about it. I could have talked to my mom or dad—they would have been understanding and sympathetic—or even to a friend. I don't know what stopped me, but I never did talk to anyone. Maybe I thought that if I showed it, if I let people know that deep down I was miserable, I would be seen as a failure at yet another thing. If only I'd known then what I know now.

My low self-confidence stopped me from doing a lot of things I wanted to do. Even as I got a little older, it stopped me from doing fun new things. When my friends suggested doing anything that was out of my comfort zone—such as taking a weekend trip to Montreal or going to Atlantic City—I was never willing to take the risk. I didn't like the idea that I wouldn't know what to expect. It made me too anxious.

I was even far too nervous to ask girls out. There were lots of girls at my school that I would have loved to talk to, but I was too scared of what they might think of me, of how much it would hurt if they rejected me. It was a completely defeatist attitude.

I started smoking in grade nine too. It started out as a few smokes here and there, usually with a beer, but it quickly became a part of my daily routine. Within a matter of months, I was smoking a pack of day, and more if I was drinking. I smoked with coffee in the morning, waiting for the bus, before school, between classes, at lunch, after school...whenever I could. I continued to smoke like that for about a decade.

One of the best things about high school was when I got my driver's license. I was sixteen. That night, I asked my mom if I could borrow her car. Not five miles from my destination, I got my first speeding ticket. It was the first of many! I quickly discovered the thrill of driving fast. It was fun, and like so many other teenagers, I was reckless.

What I wanted more than anything was a car of my own. I had a job cleaning stalls at a local barn, so I saved all my money with the hopes of eventually finding a car I loved. One day, I spied an old muscle car for sale, sitting out in a farmer's field. I fell in love. It was a bright orange, 4-speed, '69 Camaro with a white interior, and it was in good shape. It was so cool. My dad drove me out there to talk with the farmer. I'd saved up almost enough money to afford it, and I asked my dad to lend me the difference. He thought about it for a week—during which time I was on pins and needles—and then he decided to help me out. I was so happy!

My car became my new hobby. If I'd put even *half* the time I put into fixing up that car into studying, I probably would have made the dean's list. I tinkered with it every chance I got. Over the next couple of years I souped it up as best I could, with the help of my dad and a friend of mine who worked as a mechanic out in Kempville. He found a great motor for me, and before long, I saved up enough to switch out the old motor for a more powerful one. I tinkered with the engine, the muffler, and the body too. My father and I spent lots of time together working on that car.

But I was also very foolish. I drove too fast and I drove heedlessly. I'd speed down country roads at over 150 kph. I thought I was indestructible and I loved drag racing. My buddy Robbie had a '69 Camaro too: his was lime green.

Robbie, Dave, Greg, Footy, and I spent countless nights racing our cars.

We'd drive out to an informal drag strip located on a stretch of road outside Ottawa. Back then, it was still a country road. It appeared deserted until you drove out far enough, when all of a sudden you could see tons of parked cars: Camaros, Mustangs, Corvettes, old Buick convertibles. There'd be a guy standing out on the road with a flag. When he dropped that flag, you better believe we were all ready to race.

By the time I was seventeen, I'd lost my licence more than once and had been stopped by the police more times than I could count. There was this one cop, Constable Seguay, who used to catch me all the time. Man, was I ever scared of him! He was actually a really good cop and a nice guy, but in my mind, he was the epitome of *policeman*. He was tall and striking and reminded me of the mirror-sunglasses-wearing trooper you would see on TV. Every time he caught me speeding, he'd tell me to smarten up, but of course I never listened.

At one point, my family had some things stolen from our barn up the road. They filed a police report, and about a week, later Constable Seguay showed up at our place. I answered the door and he looked down at me and smiled. I shook in my boots. I was sure he had come to tell my parents what a brat I was! He asked if my parents were home, and I called for my mom. Constable Seguay looked down at me and grinned. I knew it was all over: I'd be grounded for months. But when my mom showed up, the Constable didn't say a thing about me. He'd come about the stolen goods from our barn. He could have told my parents all kinds of things, but he didn't. I never forgot that.

By grade twelve, I had made friends with a group of kids

who were all really creative—the artsy kids at school. I remember being really impressed by their passion. I enjoyed their company because I appreciated what they did and I found comfort in their optimism. I figured if I couldn't be passionate and creative myself, at least I could be around it. Part of what interested me about this group what that it seemed like they had a clear sense of who they were and what they wanted out of life. I respected that. I don't think it occurred to me back then that their sense of themselves was exactly what I appreciated about them. I didn't even know it, but I wished I had some idea of my own identity and purpose. Even though I had lots of different groups of friends, I never felt that I fit in anywhere.

I wanted to be good at something. I loved riding horses, so in my late teens, I started to enter riding competitions. I wasn't *bad* at it— I knew that much—but I didn't have any confidence in myself as a competitor. I eventually started going to horse shows on the weekend. Those shows were mostly in the eastern provinces, usually in Quebec or Ontario. I had a great horse I rode named Barbie, and I met lots of cool people in the industry. I won a few competitions too. It was gratifying to win, but even placing on the podium wasn't good enough for me. I was always beating myself up for not being better. If I didn't place 1st, I felt like a failure. I wanted to be the best and I put a lot of pressure on myself. It just made me anxious and miserable.

It wasn't just the anxiety. Going to horse shows meant that I had to travel a lot. That seemed great at first. I got to see places in Canada I'd never been before. But by the time summer rolled around, I felt like I was missing out on everything my friends were doing. They were probably going out to cottages, having parties, fishing, racing…I missed it all. I felt so disconnected from life at home.

Eventually, I broke down. The pressure I'd put on myself was too intense and I couldn't take it anymore. I quit riding and went home.

Looking back on it, I felt terrible about quitting. In some ways, I think I set myself up for failure. When I was riding, I felt bad because I didn't think I was good enough. When I stopped, I felt bad because I'd quit. I ignored it.

Towards the end of high school, I met my first girlfriend. Her name was Jen, and she went to one of the neighbouring schools. We were introduced to each other through a mutual friend. She was very pretty, with dark olive skin and curly blond hair, and she was nice. I don't just mean *nice* the way people say it all the time. I mean she was *genuinely* nice. She had a knack for making the people around her feel comfortable. I felt like I could really be myself around her. It took me a long time to get up the nerve to ask her out, and when I finally did, she politely declined. But I liked her too much to take no for an answer. I kept asking until she finally agreed to go out with me. Before long, we were an item. It was total puppy love.

# CHAPTER THREE

Running from My Life
The Early '90s

The year after I graduated from high school, I enrolled at Algonquin College. It was convenient for me because it was close to my parents place and a couple of my friends were going there. I wasn't really that inspired; going to college was just what I was expected to do, so I did it. What I liked most about the school was the social aspect. There were tons of new people to meet and lots of parties to go to. I made a lot of new friends. I'd never been shy, that's for sure, but in college, I got more comfortable with the idea of meeting new people and trying new things.

After deliberating for a while, I decided to take the three-year business administration program. I didn't know what else to take. Rob and I had started a small landscaping company when we were still teenagers, so I figured business administration might be a logical step forward for me. I went to my classes and gave it the old farmer's try, but I never excelled. Maybe academia was never for me. That's definitely what I thought at the time.

The first few years of college were fun. I wouldn't say that I lived a bad-boy lifestyle exactly, but I wasn't a saint either. I remember doing some pretty silly things, like the time a bunch of buddies and I ran a rope from a certain fast-food company's plastic statue to the back of the car and then dragged the poor thing 160 kph down the highway, or the time that Greg and I skipped classes for several days so that we could drive out to an outdoor music festival.

We were kids. We partied. Life was about having fun.

But out of nowhere, tragedy struck in three.

After being diagnosed with lung cancer, my grandfather died. We don't know where the cancer came from for sure, but he had worked in the steel mill his whole life. It was a very difficult time for the whole family. It was very hard for me to understand how a man who had always been so strong and robust could become so weak and frail in so short a time. It was my first real experience with death.

It must have been especially hard on my grandmother. They'd had a wonderfully strong marriage. They were best friends. I couldn't even begin to imagine the pain that she must have felt when she lost him. She told us that right before he'd passed away, in the hospital, he'd grabbed her wrist and told her that he was scared to go.

"Don't be scared," she said, but we don't know if he heard her, because those were his last words. She was inconsolable.

My uncle Tom was terribly grieved by his passing. He was the youngest of three siblings and the only boy. The two of them had been very close.

Almost a year to the day that my grandfather died, Uncle Tom was killed. He had been on his tractor, clearing some brush, when the tractor flipped over and killed him. No one could believe it. It was too much for us to handle.

I realized how fragile our lives are. I'd had no real concept of death, of how easily we could lose our loved ones or even our own lives. Uncle Tom hadn't even been sick; at just thirty-eight, he was a healthy young man! It was so random. And my grandfather, who seemed so strong and healthy himself, had been hit with a disease that took over his body in a matter of months. None of it made sense.

When I thought that things couldn't get any worse, my father had a stroke that changed his life forever. He was out with a friend when it happened. They got him to the hospital in time to save his life, but by then the damage was already done.

My father's stroke signalled the end of an era to me. There had been so much death and sadness around us. I knew our family would never be the same again. We used to go to Ohio every summer for big family get-togethers, but I knew that was over. Too much of the family was suddenly gone.

So this is what life is like, I remember thinking. I can't say I was impressed. I was angry after all that. The men in my family were disappearing and the father I had known was gone too. Things seemed incredibly fucked up. Life seemed like a series of tragedies and disappointments.

Before his stroke, my dad was a very happy man. He loved his job and his life, but everything changed afterwards. He was no longer able to perform surgery. He couldn't even be self-sufficient. His whole right side didn't function properly. The things he was used to doing on his own he couldn't do without help anymore, even the simplest of things: driving, tying his shoes, working on the car. He couldn't even get up the stairs anymore, and so he slept down in the family room. His personality changed. He became quiet. He seemed unhappy and disinterested. I could understand. He'd lost the life he'd loved.

His depression had a major effect on all of us at home. It was as if he wasn't our dad anymore. The man who had taught us so much, the man who had been vivid and extroverted, the man who'd always had the right answers was gone for a period of time. At first, it was like we were living with a stranger. We never knew what he was thinking or how he might react. Life was unpredictable. It was a struggle to reacquaint ourselves with our father and to relearn how to make him happy. It was very difficult to see him so unhappy and generally disinterested.

Our house no longer seemed like our home. It wasn't the happy peaceful sanctuary I'd grown up in. I didn't like being there anymore. I knew my mother needed help, so I didn't want to move out, but I tried to stay out as much as possible.

Jen was a great comfort to me. Since the end of high school, we had been growing apart. She was more mature than I, and her idea of a big night out on the town wasn't an impromptu drag race. But that still didn't change the fact that she cared about my family and me. Jen had a big heart and she wanted to be there for me. She did her best, but our relationship was crumbling. When we broke up, I took it really hard. I couldn't let the relationship go. I felt sorry for myself. It seemed like another failure.

I think that's when I really turned to alcohol. It's not like I didn't drink before, because I did. College was all about partying. But after my father's stroke, it got a lot worse. I wanted to get my mind off things. There was an endless stream of parties to attend, and I'd go from one to the next, often crashing at a buddy's house instead of going home at night.

Maybe I was hoping to find happiness at the bottom of a bottle. Maybe I thought I could run away from my own life. I'm not sure. I wasn't thinking about it at the time. All I knew was that I liked to drink. I didn't want to analyze it any further.

I exhibited a complete lack of respect for myself. I didn't care what I was doing to my grades. I didn't care what I looked like. I didn't care whether I was messing up my future. Whenever those kinds of thoughts came into my head, I'd push them out. I didn't want to deal with it. I just wanted to grab another beer, another bottle of whiskey, and drink until I puked. In those days, I could drink myself sober. Enough was *never* enough.

Strangely, even after losing my grandfather and my uncle, I still didn't really give any thought to my own mortality, and I was too wrapped up in my own life to think about the lives of others. I still went drag racing all the time, and I'd get behind the wheel after drinking too. But one day, I had a very close call. It changed a few of my bad habits for good.

I was driving down the Queensway late one night in my mom's car. I looked out in my rear-view mirror and saw the lights of another car behind me. The next thing I remember is catching a glimpse of my dashboard, which was cracked straight down the middle.

I'd been hit so hard that my car had cruised down the road several hundred feet. It slammed through signs and whatever else was in its way, and then flipped over onto its side. That's how I was found. The car was completely totalled. The police told me it was a miracle I wasn't killed.

They later found the guy who hit me. A drunk driver. I was so mad at him. But then I realized that I had got behind the wheel without being sober on more than one occasion myself. What if it had been me that hit someone? What if I had hurt or even killed someone? What if I killed myself? I knew how lucky I was, and decided I didn't want to test my luck anymore. I quit drinking and driving, and shortly after that, I stopped drag racing too.

I never actually graduated from college. I was close, but I was missing a course. I could have gone back and taken the extra credit, but I didn't want to. I was sick of school— sick of studying for classes I didn't care about. I just stopped going. I can't say for certain, but when our graduation ceremony occurred, I was probably at the bar.

# CHAPTER FOUR

Messin' with Texas
1994 – 1995

After college, I worked as a landscaper, but in truth, I was aimless. There's no other way to describe it. Nothing inspired me, nothing motivated me. In fact, the only thing I remember taking seriously was my car and my beer. I loved my car. I loved my beer.

It's not like I was eighteen anymore. I was twenty-four years old. I was a college dropout acting like a teenager. I'd attend parties whenever I heard about them, doing whatever it took, drinking whatever it took, to silence the ugly voice in my head that kept berating me. You're not good enough, it said. You're not doing anything with your life. You're a fuck-up, it told me. I didn't want to hear it, so I partied it away. Sometimes it worked. Most of the time it didn't. But I was good at keeping it all inside. Whatever was going on in my head, I kept to myself. On the outside, I looked like a happy-go-lucky dude, and none of my friends were the wiser.

In the spring of my twenty-fourth year, an old buddy of mine came to see me. Since college, Bill had gone on to become a computer programmer. I didn't want to admit it to myself, but I felt a bit jealous of his success. It's not that I didn't think he deserved it, because he did. It's just that his life looked like it had a trajectory. I couldn't even imagine what I'd be doing in ten years.

We went to my favourite bar, the Heart and Crown, and as we were having a beer, he brought up a subject that I'd been avoiding for years.

"Hey," he said, "have you ever thought about riding again?"

I guess I had entertained the thought a few times, but I didn't want to do it. I'd already quit, and that had been hard enough.

"No way. Absolutely not," I told him. "I'll never ride again."

"Well, look," Bill told me, "a buddy of mine has some horses and they need some help. Why don't you think about it? Give it a try?"

Bill had my best intentions in mind, but I knew what would happen. I knew that if I were to get back on a horse, I'd get sucked right back into that world. It was almost like an addiction.

But the more I thought about it, the more I couldn't justify refusing. Besides, I reasoned, it wasn't like I was being asked to ride again. This was different: I'd *train* the horses. Maybe that's what I was meant to do after all. I liked the idea of having purpose, of putting the knowledge I had to good use.

I went out to the farm and tried out one of the horses Bill's friend owned. The second I saddled up, I realized that I *did* miss riding. Almost immediately, I was able to correct some of the issues the other trainers were having trouble with, and it felt good to help. It didn't take much time before I had a whole bunch of clients. I gave riding lessons and trained the horses. Being back in the saddle felt comfortable. Then something really remarkable happened. I received a call one day from a friend of a friend: a guy who was in touch with Terry Thompson, a legendary horse trainer and a childhood hero of mine!

In our brief phone conversation, he told me that he could hook me up with a job as an assistant trainer down on Terry's ranch in Texas. I was shocked! Here I was, not even pursuing it, and a major opportunity just landed in my lap. I felt like a player in the minor leagues being called up to the majors. I was psyched, to say the least.

It didn't take much thinking on my part. If I was going to train horses, I might as well train under the best. As a kid, it had been my dream to be a cowboy. Now I really would be one, and in Texas too. I decided to leave Canada and everything I knew behind. I felt bad leaving my parents behind, but my father had been getting a lot better and I thought my mom would be okay without me. The consequences of my father's stroke would never go away, but he had readjusted to life in his own way. I packed my bags, said goodbye, and prepared myself for the beginning of a whole new life.


One of the ranch owners, Susan Brainard, picked me up at the Fort Worth airport. We headed to Aubrey, which is about forty minutes away from the airport in North Central Texas. As we were driving along, I was amazed at how big the sky looked. It seemed like the horizon never ended. It was so different from any place I'd seen before. Texas was flat as a desert. You could see way, way off into the distance and I liked that immediately.

On the way to the ranch, we stopped off at a tack and feed store so Susan could pick up a couple of supplies. As I walked around the store, I was amazed by how much *stuff* was in there. Everything and anything that had to do with horses was in there. That was when I realized how enormous the equestrian industry in Texas is. It really is part of the fabric of the place.

When we got back in the car, I was a little overwhelmed.

"Wow," I said to Susan, "there must be a lot of people who ride in Texas!"

Susan laughed. I guess in Texas that goes without saying.

"See now," she said, "if you're a boy growin' up around here, you got two choices in life: be a cowboy or play football."

I laughed but I also knew it was probably true.

I rolled down the window and smelled the Texas air. It reminded me, for some reason, of potatoes. I could feel the heat even though we were driving and the open window created a breeze. It really was hot. I mean, *really* hot—fry eggs on the hood of your car hot. It didn't take long for me to realize that no matter how hot it got I still liked it. Even dressed in heavy jeans and all my riding gear, the heat made me feel good.

Terry Thompson looked like a cowboy, talked like a cowboy, and, man, did he ever ride like one! He was a large man, with the kind of face that looked like he'd been working hard every day of his life. But if his exterior was slightly intimidating, the man himself was just the opposite: he was a smart, generous, funny kind of dude, and I knew right away that we would get along just fine. I had looked up to him as a kid. When I met the man in person, I knew that he would still be a hero to me.

I went to the ranch to train reining horses. Reining is a western kind of riding competition (akin to, but not the same as dressage). It was a departure from what I had done at home, but I knew that with some instruction from Terry and a little bit of time to familiarize myself with the style, I would get the hang of it. I'm comfortable around horses, and I respect and admire them. I think that a trainer needs to feel that way if he hopes to have any success in the field. We were dealing with quarter horses mostly, a really versatile compact horse and some of the fastest sprinters out there. Hence the name: quarter horses originally raced quarter miles.

The Diamond B Ranch—which is what it was called at the time—was a truly amazing place. The ranch itself must have been worth millions of dollars. It was enormous and sat on acres and acres of land, most of which was riding facility. It was so huge and self-sufficient that apart from picking up groceries and feed, you really never had to leave if you didn't want to. We had both indoor and outdoor facilities, and there were several barns. The biggest one had more than a hundred stalls. But I just liked being outside. There were miles and miles of land. There were trees, ponds, sun, and sky as far as the eye could see.

There were about five houses on the property. I moved into one with two other assistant trainers. One of them, to my surprise, was another Canadian. It was a treat to meet Leslie and to find a little bit of home so far away. I discovered soon enough that we'd both be getting a share of teasing about our accents. I can't remember how many times someone would ask us to say "out and about" or "sorry" and then try to mimic the way we said it. As if *we* didn't think *their* gab was weird enough! But it was all in good fun.

I also met Leslie's boyfriend, and I'll never be able to forget him. Like just about everyone on the ranch, he was suited up like a true cowboy. He had the Wranglers, the hat, the spurs, the boots, the whole nine yards. Looking at him, I thought he was a born and bred Texan. That was why I was so surprised when he opened his mouth and I discovered that he didn't speak a word of English! He was actually from Italy, and had come to the ranch to have some horses trained. We couldn't talk, but beer and food is an international language, and in that way, we got along just fine.

We had a small lake right beside the house, where I used

to like to go out and fish every once in a while. I'd been warned that there were water moccasins out there, and that they were really poisonous, so I knew I had to be careful. One afternoon, with my jeans tucked into my boots, I tried to make my way through the waist-high grass that surrounded the water. I heard rustling in the grass, and when I looked out at the water, I saw a snake! I knew they were venomous, but I'd never seen one. It was bigger than any snake I'd seen, and I didn't like the look on its face. It was swimming towards me with most of its body above the water. I hightailed it out of there before we a chance to be formally introduced!

We worked really hard all day on the ranch—harder than I was used to working back home. At night, we'd relax and build a bonfire or go out to one of the nearby honky-tonks. I'd always had a predilection for country and western music, but my tastes ran more towards the stuff my uncle Tom had played for me in Ohio. At the ranch, however, whenever I put a CD on, it would be turned off almost immediately. I was informed on more than one occasion that the only music we'd be listening to while we rode our horses together would be either George Strait or Bob Wills. It didn't take long before I had all their lyrics down pat.

Although I didn't entirely quit drinking in Texas, I did slow it down some. We had so much work to do and I was constantly busy, so there wasn't time to drink. Being on the ranch was a totally new level of professionalism for me—we lived and breathed horses. I'd wake up very early in the morning and feed the horses. After that, I'd clean the stalls and prepare Terry's first horse of the day. Then I'd saddle up my own first horse and get it ready to ride.

Sometimes I'd ride up to nineteen horses in one day. I'd be rubbed so raw from riding that my inner thighs would be completely chaffed and covered in blisters. I'd wrap them in what seemed like miles of gauze. Worse than that, the constant riding would take a serious toll on my back. I had gone through periods of time where I lifted weights in an attempt to strengthen the muscles in my back and ward off some of the pain, but I guess I didn't do enough. My back and hips were always in pain. But that was the deal, and I told myself it was worth it. At the end of a long day of training, I would cool out Terry's horses, and then mine, and later I would feed and clean them again.

The reason why I would prepare Terry's horses in the morning is because everyday, without fail, he would get up at the crack of dawn to go running. He'd sometimes run past me when I was leaning up against the wall of the barn, having a smoke. I thought it was hilarious and I'd tease him about it.

"Where the hell are you going, Terry? There's no time to jog! We've got horses to ride!" I'd yell.

Without breaking pace, Terry would yell back at me, "One day you gotta quit those cigarettes, kid!"

His words went in one ear out the next. I'd laugh and finish my smoke, butt it out on the ground, and turn in to the barn. Quit smoking? That was out of the question for me. I smoked a pack a day, and I couldn't imagine myself as a non-smoker. I loved smoking. I loved the taste of a smoke first thing in the morning and a cigarette with a cold beer. Quit smoking? No way. Lung cancer? Whatever.

And running? That didn't make a lick of sense in my mind. Why would Terry be bothered? After all, he could always go riding.

One of my favourite things about the ranch was lunchtime. Every afternoon, Susan Brainard would invite all of the assistant trainers to the main house. There were about seven of us, and she always managed to lay out a cool spread: fajitas, real Southern barbeque, chili. I loved it!

Apart from the food, another great thing was that I got to ride with the best. I met people I had looked up to as a kid, and sometimes I got to ride with them. Once, an Olympic-level dressage rider came to the ranch to ride with Terry and it was exhilarating for me. I loved watching them and always felt like I was getting some of the best hands-on experience I could ever hope for. Hey, if you're going to learn, why not learn from the best?

I *was* learning from the best. Riding with Terry was like a dream come true. But sometimes, when I was alone at night, I would start to think about what I was really doing out there. Was this it? It was great—but was this it?

It wasn't until after about five months in Texas that I started to feel really comfortable there. I was a part of a community, and I was learning a ton. But I was also really missing home. I knew that staying in Texas meant that I'd have a good job, but I missed my country. Being away from home actually made me feel a sense of national identity that I'd never felt so strongly before. I really felt *Canadian* and that I ought to be there, not in the States. It was hard for me to leave Texas: I'd made some good friends and had the chance to work with someone I truly admired. But I wanted to go home.

# CHAPTER FIVE

Home Sweet Home
1995 – 1998

It felt great to be home. It's easy to take for granted the sights, smells, and sounds you experience on a daily basis, but there's nothing like being gone for a while to remind you how much you truly appreciate them. I guess Dorothy had it right: there really is no place like home.

I was so happy to see my brother, my parents, and all my friends again. I couldn't wait to do the simple things such as drive my car and go to my favourite restaurants. The food in Texas was good, there's no doubt about that, but by then I'd had enough pulled pork to last me a lifetime.

The downside of coming home was that I was broke. I'd been able to save something of a nest egg while I was in Texas, but I came home with the intention of building a horse training business of my own. I wanted to take everything I had learned on the ranch and apply it to my own business. That was going to cost money. A lot of money.

I moved back in with my parents. I have to admit, it was kind of demoralizing. None of my friends lived at home anymore, and even my younger brother had moved out of the house. Many of my friends owned their own houses by then. I had to fight the urge to beat myself up. I'd taken a risk by going to Texas and I'd learned a lot. I tried to tell myself it was just a minor setback.

Even if I wasn't thrilled by the idea of living at home, things there really weren't bad at all. My mother and father had found a routine that worked for them, and my father had recovered from the stroke as best he could. I didn't find the atmosphere as depressing as before. It made me very happy to see my father finally finding some joy in his life. He was back to practicing medicine, and although he still could not perform operations, he was consulting on surgeries. Things weren't as good as they had been when I was growing up— that time had come and gone—but his condition was old hat for all of us now and we all learned to deal with it as best we could. It became normal.

In terms of my business, I think it's fair to say that things started off with a bang. Within several months, I had an impressive list of clients. I leased three stables, and I looked after horses in other barns. I even kept a few horses in my parents' old barn. I worked my butt off every day. It paid off too: my list of clients grew and grew. The only problem was I still wasn't turning a profit. By the end of the second year, although I was incredibly busy, I still wasn't making enough money to move out of my parents' house. I rode all day, and if I wasn't riding, I was in transit, getting from one barn to another.

It wasn't long before I started developing personal training programs for my clients as well. It made sense to do so: if they were stronger and more physically fit, they would be better equipped to ride their horses. I found I liked designing training programs, and most of my clients were a pleasure to work with.

Of course, as with any business, there's always going to be a few bad eggs in the bunch. I had a few clients who were difficult to deal with. This didn't bother me at first, but as time went on, it started to wear on me. Problem clients became harder to cope with. Explaining that I wasn't a miracle worker became more and more frustrating. Perhaps more than anything, it hurt me to see certain clients put so much pressure on their horses that it seemed to suck the soul out of the animals. The pressure an owner can put on their horse can be extremely intense. It broke my heart to see it.

I had a lot of my buddies around, and we'd often go out drinking together. Even though I never vented any of my frustrations about the job to them, going out with my pals was one way of blowing off steam. But maybe I blew off a little too much steam—when you wake up in the morning with a splitting headache and feel like you're about to heave, you know you've overdone it. I overdid it a lot.

During my years as a horse trainer in Ottawa, I had the chance to work with two of my all-time favourite horses. When you work with horses for a long time, you begin to think of them as friends. I worked with two that were like real buddies to me.

One was a Canadian Sport Horse named Orion, a beautiful, strong, majestic animal. He was dark bay coloured and probably the biggest horse I've ever ridden, about seventeen hands. Orion could turn a bad day around. We got on extremely well. I believe we had an emotional bond. He used to start running around in his paddock when he saw me. We trained together for a long time and I'm very proud to say that he went on to win some major competitions after our time together.

My other best bud was a little Appaloosa stallion by the name of Prince. He stayed in one of the barns I leased, and he was the cutest horse I ever knew. Prince was a tiny little guy, white with black dots, and his tail was so long it actually trailed on the ground. These two horses made my days worthwhile, and I looked forward to riding them every day.

Looking after all the horses I had in my care was an enormous responsibility. I would get up when the sky was still dark and travel to the various barns to feed them and do stable work. Then I trained them. I rode all day. At night, I did the same series of chores in reverse. I could never be far from the horses for any length of time, and I began to envy my friends with secure jobs, who would go in to the office in the morning and then leave their work and responsibility there for the night.

As time went on, the business caused me more and more anxiety. I'd wake up in the morning with a pit in my stomach, thinking about whether any of the owners were at the barn before me. What if they were? Surely they'd be complaining about me not being there yet.

The anxiety because more intense. To make matters worse, I wasn't making any money. Between the feed and hay bills and the cost of leasing the barns, I was lucky if I broke even in any given month. More often than not I lost money.

I had come back to Canada with big dreams. I'd envisioned myself as an entrepreneur. I liked the idea of working for myself and not answering to a boss. But all told, I didn't feel like I was working for myself at all. In fact, it was the opposite. I felt like I had a hundred bosses—one for each of the horses I looked after. I was stressed out. I couldn't stop thinking the same thing: here I am doing my best and I *still* can't make it work.

One night, I was out at the Heart and Crown with a bunch of my friends. It was a Friday night and the place was packed. I knew almost everyone in the room.

It was a convivial atmosphere—people were laughing and talking and joking around, usually the kind of thing that could get me out of a funk. The Stones pumped through the bar's speakers. A couple of my friends had just seen their favourite hockey team score on the TV above the bar, and they were feeling upbeat and rowdy. My friend Brian came and sat next to me.

"What's up, buddy?"

I tried to act like everything was cool. I was pretty good at faking it.

"Oh, nothing man, I'm just a little tired. Nothing a few beers can't fix," I replied.

Looking at me, you might have thought I was feeling great, that everything was coming up roses. I didn't want to tell anyone what I was really thinking as I pounded back those beers. Some familiar song came on the jukebox, one of those old favourites that people always sing along to. It was the strangest thing, I was sitting there with a smoke in one hand and a beer in the other, singing along with the whole drunken bar and looking as happy as the next guy. But inside I was thinking something totally different. I was thinking that I was a fool to drop out of college, that I should've picked up a skill or trade, that I should have lived my whole life differently.

That night, I finally allowed myself to admit that no matter how much I loved horses I didn't love the business. All of a sudden, I saw myself for what I really was: broke, bored, and unhappy. My life felt so empty, so aimless. It was like one big "so what?"

I'd wanted to be a cowboy all my life, and now I was one. Be careful what you wish for, I guess, because deep down, I knew I didn't want to do it anymore. Is this really it, I thought, is *this* the life I have?

# CHAPTER SIX

Epiphanies on Bar Stools
1998 – 1999

Up until I started running, most of my major life decisions were made sitting on a bar stool at the Heart and Crown. When I allowed myself to look honestly at my life, I was able to accept the fact that I wasn't happy. I didn't push it out of my mind and suppress it as I had done so many times before. However, just owning that didn't really change much, and it took me more than a year to really modify the way I lived.

After that night at the Heart and Crown, I started playing around with the idea of becoming a personal trainer. I had already been doing something like personal training with a few of my riding clients, and I wanted to take it a step further. I also liked the idea of working with people. I began to read up on the subject, and at the same time, I started tapering off my riding clients. I didn't tell anyone I wouldn't be training horses anymore. Perhaps I wasn't ready to admit that I wanted to change careers. It was such a big risk. I told myself I couldn't just *stop*; I had obligations to my clients and horses and I didn't want to abandon them.

In 1998, I was hanging out at my brother's house when we happened to catch the Eco-Challenge on television. It was the coolest thing I'd ever seen on TV. I couldn't believe those people. They seemed like everything I wasn't: confident, risk-taking, determined, athletic.

I was mesmerized. I couldn't stop thinking about them. I wanted to be more like those athletes. John thought it was really cool too. We enlisted our buddy Brian, and together, the three of us decided we'd attempt an adventure race ourselves. We entered the Canadian Quest, held in the Laurentians.

We were excited about the race, but we didn't take our training seriously. In fact, what we did couldn't really be described as "training." It was more like we screwed around. We went out for a few bike rides, a couple of hikes, went rock-climbing a few times. I didn't even consider quitting smoking. I decided I'd stop smoking for the duration of the race, which was six days long.

Considering our lack of training, I'm surprised we lasted as long as we did. I don't think we stayed for two days. By the end of the second day, I was so tired I could barely move and Brian was sick. In the middle of the night, deep in the Laurentians, we decided to call it quits. It just wasn't going to happen. Besides, I was dying for a smoke! That was it for adventure racing for a couple of years.

In 1999, a year after admitting to myself that I wasn't happy with my life, I finally made up my mind to change things for good. I remember the night it happened. I was preparing to meet up with a bunch of friends at the bar. As I was getting ready, I had a little conversation with myself.

"So what are you doing?" I asked myself.

"I'm getting ready to go out."

"What are you going to do when you're out?"

"Well, I'm going to drink ten pints or so."

"Then what?"

"Then I'm probably going to be sick."

"Then what?"

"Then I'm going to go home and feel like crap and wake up with a hangover."

I didn't like what I heard, but at least I was being honest with myself. I was so predictable. A few hours later, I found myself sitting at the bar. Again. I felt horrible.

I sat there smoking my face off and drinking one beer after the next. As I looked back over my college years, it occurred to me that all of my friends had moved on with their lives. Even the buddies I was with at the bar were establishing their lives. They had futures. Where was mine?

And then it hit me. It was a personal revelation. Why was I always doing this to myself? Instead of complaining and being upset, and internalizing all this unhappiness, why didn't I actually do something about it? Why didn't I stop worrying about what I *should* be doing and just do *something*? I decided that even if I couldn't control anything else about my life, I could at the very least control my own level of physical fitness. It seemed like the right place to start.

That night, I decided I would quit smoking. It was the very first step I committed to. Even as I sat there, mulling all this stuff over, with a smoke in my mouth, I knew that I had to give it up. I wanted to set a date. The new millennium was fast approaching: I decided my very last cigarette would be on New Year's Eve. It gave me a couple of months to get used to the idea and to prepare myself. I'd smoked for over ten years. It wasn't going to be easy, but I wasn't going to allow myself to dwell on that.

I also decided that I was going to quit training horses once and for all. No more tapering off, as I had been doing for the last year. No more *thinking* about it without doing anything. No more being scared of the big "what ifs." I gave myself the same deadline for that too: January 1, 2000.

I didn't tell anyone about the decisions I made that night. I didn't make any drunken declarations. I simply resolved to train myself—mind and body—to do everything opposite to the way I'd done it before. How I'd been going about things obviously didn't work, so I decided to try the opposite. If I was used to thinking cold, I'd think hot. If I was used to thinking white, I'd think black.

The more I thought about it, the more confident I felt. I was done feeling bad all the time, done thinking of myself as a failure. I wanted to make something happen. I wanted to leave my old life behind and see what was on the other side.

I steeled myself against a weak will. I challenged myself. And assuming the world didn't blow up come the new year, things *were* going to change.

# CHAPTER SEVEN

New Year's Eve 1999

My friends and I all decided to go to the Congress Centre for New Year's Eve. I'd spent the last couple of months gearing up for the night. I wanted to cut back on my drinking and quit smoking entirely. It would all begin on January 1, 2000.

I was actually excited. When we walked into the party, I took a deep breath. All right, I said to myself, this is it. This is your last chance to party, so enjoy it while it lasts.

The atmosphere that night was electric. Y2K was on everyone's mind, and you could feel it in the air. Everyone wanted to have the best night of their lives, in case it turned out to be their last. I was no exception, and I was in high spirits.

When someone came over the loudspeaker to announce that there were only five minutes left before the countdown to the new millennium, my stomach did a little flip. I was standing by myself at the time. I pulled out my final cigarette. All right, I told myself, here it comes.

I lit it up and started smoking. I wanted to enjoy every last drop of that cigarette. I was still sucking on my smoke when the final countdown to 2000 started. Everyone was cheering and counting down together.

*…ten…nine…eight…*

I told myself that this was the countdown to the beginning of the rest of my life. I liked that idea. It seemed full of possibilities.

*…seven…six…five…*

I smoked that cigarette down to the nub.

*…four…three…two…*

I threw my smoke down on the floor and butt it out with my foot. I told myself to remember that image—that symbolism—because I knew it was going to be a long hard process. But I also knew that as long as I kept with it I would be happier and stronger for it.

*…one!*

The crowd went crazy. It wasn't just *any* new year; it was a new millennium! Everything was fresh and new. I felt good. I was ready to change.

# CHAPTER EIGHT

My Own Story
2000

Quitting smoking was about as difficult as I expected it to be. It's never easy. I went cold turkey. The first couple of days were the worst! I was cranky and all out of sorts. I kept reminding myself that eventually the agony would disappear, and when it did, I would have reached my goal. I wanted to smoke, but I wanted to quit even more.

Each day, I became more determined, more focused. Once a week had gone by, the cravings became less severe. After two weeks, I was starting to feel like a non-smoker. It was amazing. I had smoked for so long, wasted so much money, had damaged my body, and all it took was a couple of weeks of discomfort. It was absolutely worth it.

My brother suggested we go ice climbing together at Calabogie Hills. I'd been rock climbing a couple of times in the '90s and always liked it well enough, so I figured I'd give ice climbing a try.

When we got there, I remember staring up at what looked like a huge curtain of ice. I couldn't believe we were actually going to climb that. Attempting to get my crampons and ice axes into the ice was amazingly difficult. It was so hard to get up; it required so much skill and strength. I dealt with it by reminding myself that this was the first real challenge of my new life. Eventually, I did it. It felt amazing. I was hooked! (No pun intended.) John and I started going climbing on a regular basis.

It was so much fun that we decided to plan a hiking and climbing trip in Scotland. John had been to the United

Kingdom the year before and returned with stories about how beautiful it was. I wanted to go too.

We planned to go in the spring. During the months leading up to our trip, I started to watch what I ate. I had already quit smoking and was drinking much less. It was the first time I could really say that I was in training. I enjoyed this newfound athleticism. I was developing a passion for the outdoors. For the first time in my life, I was starting to think positive. I was surprised to find that my negative thoughts were becoming weaker. They hadn't disappeared entirely, but there seemed to be a battle going on between the two, and it looked like the optimistic side was winning.

I was so excited to go overseas—I'd never been anywhere else besides the States! We flew to Glasgow and then rented a car. John and I started to make our way to Glen Coe, where we were going to rent a room in a small bed and breakfast.

On our way to Glen Coe, I fell asleep. When I woke, we were in the Highlands. I was so amazed at the contrast from where I lived. I'd seen big skies in Texas, but this was something else. There were no trees! It was all rock and mountains. It looked almost barren, and yet I thought the simplicity was beautiful. I didn't know it at the time, but I would continue to be attracted to simple landscapes.

As we drove along towards the B&B, the mountains kept getting bigger. John pulled into a tourist parking area off the road. He grabbed his pack.

"Let's go climb that one," he said, referring to a great big mountain to our left. "C'mon," he said. "Right now!"

At first, I thought he must be crazy. We'd just been on a long flight and then been driving for two hours. But then I thought, why the hell not? We're here, and we might as well!

We didn't use our guidebook; we just scrambled up the

side of the mountain. It was physically gruelling for me! John was way ahead of me, and had no trouble at all. He was in excellent shape. On the other hand, my lungs felt like they were going to give out. I wondered if I'd quit smoking too late—maybe I'd already done too much damage. Eventually though, after a whole lot of huffing and puffing, we made our way up to the very top.

There I was, at the top of a mountain. We must have been thousands of feet up. I looked way off into the distance at the rolling hills and all the greenery. It felt so good. Not only did it *feel* amazing, but it was a *measurable* success! I'd been at the bottom of the mountain, and now I was at the top. I'd never been to the top before. It was the first time I'd ever done anything like that, and I felt rewarded by a feeling of such fulfilment and achievement. I felt like a light had been turned on inside me. I was so stoked! It was as if every layer of the old me was being peeled away. I couldn't wait to see what the rest of the trip would bring.

The B&B was amazing. It was inexpensive and the woman who ran the place was very hospitable. She was quite a character, and treated us like long lost sons. Every morning, she cooked us a huge breakfast of eggs, sausage, bacon, tomatoes, baked beans, oatcakes, and toast and jam. Because we were on such a tight budget, we would fill ourselves up to the brim: it would be our only full meal of the day.

"Have you had enough, boys?" she would say.

"Can we have some more, please?" we would both ask, like schoolboys. She was more than happy to oblige.

"Now you boys," she would say every morning before we went out for the days adventure. "Now you boys ought to notify Mountain Rescue before you go out. I'm frightened you won't return!"

But we did return, everyday, and had no need for Mountain Rescue. Hiking (or, as it's called in Scotland: walking) seemed like a very simple formula for elation for me. Every time we got to the top of a mountain, I felt a sense of discovery and happiness.

I discovered things about myself that I didn't know. I loved to push myself! I loved to face my fears! I would often find myself frozen with terror faced with the exposure, but John would encourage me to go forward. And when we had made it to the top, I couldn't believe that I'd really done it. I surprised myself by deciding to do it again and again. Everyday was a challenge, and I loved it!

On our last day in Glen Coe, John suggested that we finish our trip with a climb up the Aonach Eagach ridge. It's an incredibly rocky ridge that has two Munro summits—mountains with a height of over 3,000 feet—as well as cliffs on either side of it. The guidebook said that it was a difficult hike, but not dangerous as long as we stayed on the path. So John and I drove out to the trailhead and started scrambling up the side of the mountain. At first it was just grassy. Then it got rocky. Then it got really steep. We spied a Scot standing on some rocks a few yards away. He was wearing a plaid kilt and his Wellingtons and had a little boy with him, maybe eight or nine years old.

"Are you walking the ridge?" we asked him.

"I am. Me and my son here were going to t'walk the ridge. Would you like to come along?" he offered.

John and I were both totally into it. We started working the mountain together. We got on top of the path and then headed to the first summit. As we started to make our way down, I could see a part of the ridge where it got really narrow and steep on both sides. I knew what that meant. As we got closer to the ridge, the trail became narrower until it was about two feet wide. On either side of us, the drops to the floor of the mountain were about 2,000 feet. I was scared. The irony of it was that the boy was hopping along the trail like there was nothing to it.

John and the Scot were ahead of me as I scrambled down the trail. They called out to me and told me where to put my hands and feet. That was helpful, but I still had fear. I started to think that I had to stop. I was too scared to go forward. And then I looked down and realized: I didn't have a choice! I was stuck up there and I had no choice but to go on. So I did.

The Scot and his son were so far ahead of us that they stopped every few minutes and waited for us to catch up. Finally, we got to the last mountaintop.

"Okay, boys," the Scot said, "y'see waaaaaay down there?" He pointed his finger down the trail. There was a tiny speck of brown in the distance. "That's a pub. There's pints waiting for us down there at the bottom. But we gotta descend through this gully. Quickest way down to the pub."

John and I looked at each other. The guidebook had specifically said not to descend this gully. It was too dangerous: people had died trying to get down.

"No, no, it's safe," the Scot said. "You'll be all right, just follow me."

We did. We started going down the path. At first, it was kind of fun—like stepping on a mini rock avalanche. The rocks were giving way under our feet and we'd jump from one scree run to another, cruising down the side of the mountain. But then it started getting steeper, and eventually I couldn't see the trail when I looked down over the edge.

"Are you sure this is right?" John asked.

The Scot seemed sure of himself, and it was clear that he knew the lay of the land. There were many small rock steps and the path appeared extremely loose in places. I was at full attention. We zigzagged down the path for hours, but finally, we got to the bottom of the mountain. When I looked up at the mountain, it looked more like a rock wall than anything else.

It was the longest toughest thing I'd ever done in my life. It made me feel like I had been reprogrammed, like even my synapses were firing differently. I was no longer looking at the world through a dark tinge. All of a sudden, it seemed like there was so much opportunity in the world, so much to discover.

I stood at the bottom of the mountain as John and the Scot chatted. I felt like a kid again. If life is anything like today, I thought, what a wonderful rollercoaster! Maybe *this* is what life is supposed to like. And if it isn't, this is how I want it to be, I thought. Standing at the base of that mountain, I decided that I wanted the rest of my life to feel the way it did on that day. I wanted the adrenaline, the thrill, and the sense of discovery.

We walked over to the pub and opened the great door to find a massive room inside. It was full of climbers and people that had been trekking all day. A couple of years before that day, I might have felt uncomfortable hanging out with the outdoorsy set, but on that day, I didn't. I felt comfortable. Everyone was hanging out, talking about his or her experiences. I could identify with the people in that pub and all of their stories, because for the first time in my life, I had a story too.

# CHAPTER NINE

Learning to Ride
2000 – 2003

Shortly after I quit smoking, I also put my beloved Camaro up for sale. I told everyone I was selling it to buy gear and pay for my trip to Scotland, but that wasn't exactly true. My Camaro was a symbol to me—a symbol of the person I *used* to be. I missed that car, I still do, but I don't miss what it represented. With some of the money I made from selling it, I invested in a mountain bike. My brother had been riding for a couple years by then, and we'd gone out together a few times. Before I quit smoking, I could hardly keep up with him, but I'd always enjoyed it. I figured it was time to give it a go. I bought my bike from Greg Christie's Ski and Cycle Works, where my brother got his. Little did I know that Greg Christie would turn into a great friend and one of my biggest supporters.

As far as my professional life was going, things were coming along, though slowly. I was training a few clients of my own: people I had trained horses for. I had offered to give them free personal training sessions, and a few of them had accepted my offer. I had to start somewhere. It felt good when my clients would tell me that the programs I developed were working for them. It was the positive reinforcement that I always felt I'd needed.

I was studying for my certifications at the YMCA. I enjoyed going to the classes, but I felt that a lot of what we were learning was review for me. Really—so much of what we learned just felt natural to me. I had an excellent instructor, a man by the name of Albert. He taught me a lot about the technical aspects of being a personal trainer, but the most important thing he ever told me wasn't about fitness.

Albert explained to me that a personal trainer can know everything there is to know about physical ability and the body and about how to make someone a great athlete, but he said that if you don't have an inspiring personality, you'll never connect with your client. If you don't connect with your client, he told me, all the knowledge in the world won't help them improve. I took that to heart, and I never forgot his advice. I respected Albert immensely, so when he told me he thought I'd be a great personal trainer, it gave me a boost of confidence.

One day, I went in to see an athletic therapist for help with my sore back. I'd been working with weights to help strengthen it, but the pain was still persistent.

My physiotherapist's office was located in the same building as an athletic testing facility. After my appointment, I poked my head around the corner and walked over to the lab. I met Ken Brune there, and he suggested that I come back with my bike and do some tests. I told him that I'd just started riding, but he told me to come back anyway so I could at least get a sense of where my fitness level was. I was apprehensive, but I figured why not?

A few weeks later, I brought my bike to the lab, where we set it up on a bike trainer and bolted it into a stand. They stuck a tube into my mouth, which was attached to a computer that read my oxygen levels and determined my maximum oxygen uptake. Every three minutes they increased the resistance on the bike. They also took blood samples and did tests to determine what my maximal heart rate zones were.

When we were done, Ken seemed a little surprised.

"Ray, your $VO_2$ max is normal, but what isn't normal is that you were able to produce a very high lactate number."

Basically, he was referring to the fact that no matter how far or how fast I went, my legs did not feel a burn. Instead, they'd just sort of give out from exhaustion.

"Yeah, I always wondered about that," I said. "I think it might be my back messing with the nerves in my legs, because even when I go up a hill, my legs don't get sore. It's actually the opposite—they just get so tired they stop working."

"Jeez, Ray," Ken said, "you should start training on your bike. Like, proper training. Why don't you come and join us at the Peak Centre? We'll put you on a trainer. Let's see how you do?"

Why not? I thought. I was more than happy to give it a try. I brought my bike to the Peak Centre and started to train there. On one of my first visits, I found myself riding next to someone who looked like he was a professional athlete. He turned out to be a guy named Corey Gladish, a semi-professional road racer, and all-round cool guy.

"So, what's your sport?" Corey asked me, as we rode side-by-side at the gym.

I paused. I didn't know what to say. What *was* my sport?

"I'm a mountain bike racer," I finally said, because that's what I felt like I was. After all, I *was* training on the bike, and I had recently decided to enter some races. It was the first time I had said it, the first time I'd identified myself as an athlete. It was also the first step towards making it real.

Corey and I hit it off. He was very instrumental in my future as a mountain biker, and we even ended up doing a few races together, including the TransRockies.

I noticed during this time that there was another transition going on with my social life. I was no longer hanging out with my old buddies at the Heart and Crown, spending every weekend wasted at the bar. In fact, with the exception of Brian, I hardly saw those guys anymore. My interests were different. All I thought about was training on the bike, building my business as a personal trainer, getting more clients and my certifications, and saving up enough money to move out of my parents' house. The money aspect wasn't coming along too well, but the athletic part was moving ahead in leaps and bounds. The fears I'd once had were now being completely replaced by the desire to take on bigger risks and to challenge myself.

I had heard about the upcoming Quebec Cup Series—a bunch of mountain bike races held all over the province—and I decided that I wanted to focus on training for those. The races are held every summer. I took my training very seriously. I was on my bike two to three hours a day. After training, I went to meet with clients or to classes at the YMCA. Over the weekend, instead of pushing myself to see how many beers I could drink, I pushed myself to see how long I could ride.

The only thing that was holding me back from getting hired at a gym was my lack of certifications. Nobody was willing to hire a personal trainer without them. I continued studying at the YMCA.

One day, I met an instructor there named Brenda Hamm. As soon as she started talking, I knew that I wanted her to be my mentor. It was clear that she had vast knowledge, especially when it came to core strength. Actually, it was Brenda who was able to help me develop my own core strength and therefore help to alleviate some of the pain in my back.

Brenda did something for which I have always been grateful: She took a chance on me. When no one was willing to hire me, Brenda let me work with her in her gym at the Life Fitness Centre. I was finally working in a real fitness facility. I also continued to study at the YMCA, but, ultimately, Brenda was my biggest role model as far as personal training is concerned.

While working at the Life Fitness Centre, I had the pleasure of meeting Nancy Manning. Nancy had a major influence on my life. She was an outstanding woman who worked for the government and in her spare time taught aerobics classes at the gym. She and I got to talking, and I mentioned that I was really getting into mountain biking. Nancy mentioned that she biked sometimes too.

Little did I know that she was a world-level mountain biker! I told her that I planned to compete in the Quebec Cup Series, and Nancy was kind enough to invite me to travel along with her and her crowd that summer.

That preceding winter, I finally decided that it was time to leave my parents' house once and for all. I moved in with my friend Gary and three other roommates. We rented an old house in Chelsea, Quebec. It was a big cedar house, probably built in the '70s, with picture windows overlooking Meech Lake and the surrounding woods and a living room with a central fireplace. Alone, none of us would have been able to afford it, but between the five of us, it was manageable.

I loved living there. Gary, a biologist, was a fascinating person whose passion was wildlife. He is recognized the world over as a leading expert on migratory birds. He had stories about all the places he'd been in around the world. I loved to hear him talk about hanging off a cliff's edge to count bird eggs. There was also Jean-Yves, a road cyclist and baker, who was half tough-guy, half mystic. With his big blue eyes and long ponytail, Jean-Yves was a favourite with the ladies.

It was great to finally be out on my own, but it wasn't always easy. There were times when I didn't have the money to make rent and Gary would have to float me for the month. A lot of the time I didn't have the money to pay for my courses in personal training, and sometimes I couldn't afford groceries. It was scary. But I had amazing friends who helped me when I needed it, and I was absolutely determined not to move back home. There was no way. When I looked back over the past year, I couldn't believe how far I'd come. Things were moving forward. I wasn't the same person, and there was no turning back.

That summer, Nancy and I travelled to the Quebec Cup Series together. She was incredibly motivating and taught me so much about mountain biking. More than the races themselves, what I remember best about that summer was spending time with her and learning about her perspective on life. It was a gift.

The races were pretty tough. They were two hours long through rocky and muddy terrain. I participated in six races, and unfortunately wasn't able to complete two of them. I could stay with the other bikers during the climbs, that was never the problem, but once we got on the trail, or started on the descents, I would have trouble keeping up and would often fall behind. I would usually finish in the top 20, which is not bad for a beginner.

Another major change took place in 2002. I moved out into my own place in Chelsea. I wouldn't consider moving anywhere else. I had grown to love the community I lived in. Chelsea hosts a lot of athletes. I think they're drawn to the same things I am: the amazing beauty of the area, the small-town feel, and all the great parks to train in, not to mention our great cross-country ski networks and our proximity to the nation's capital. I love Chelsea because apart from being so beautiful, it feels like a real community. You see people you know all the time. When I'd take my bike out, I'd see my neighbours and friends all over the place. I'd wave to the mechanic on the corner, to the guy that owns the convenience store, to Cindy, who owns my favourite local coffee shop. In Chelsea, I've always felt at home.

By the end of the year, I'd had a lot of good times riding my bike, but after the Quebec Cup Series, I knew that short races weren't for me. It wasn't until nearly a full year later that someone told me about 24-hour racing. I'd heard of 24-hour races before, but I'd always thought they were done in teams of five and six. When I found out that you could do it solo, my interest was piqued. For whatever reason, I was actually attracted to the idea of sleep deprivation. I didn't really consider the physical aspect of that kind of challenge; I just thought it would be fun.

Within a week of finding out about 24-hour races, I heard about one taking place in Bromont, Quebec. It was called the 24 Hours of Bromont, and it was in conjunction with the World Masters Mountain Bike Championships. I didn't have anyone to go with me, but I wanted to give it a shot. I filled up my gearbox, sorted out my water bottles, packed a tent, and piled my bike into my truck. Off I went. I knew I'd see a bunch of people I knew, and that Nancy would be out there, but I wondered whether I could manage the race without a support team.

When I pulled into the race grounds, I saw a ton of cars. There were lots of people milling around. There were riders from around the world there because of the championships. I parked and registered, picked up my race kit, and started mingling with the other racers. I mentioned to them that I didn't have any support. Everyone was really nice, so I asked whether they would mind if I laid my bottles out with theirs and if their support crews would mind passing them to me when I came through. Nobody minded at all. The race community is really cool, and it was no big deal.

With that taken care of, I set up my tent, and after spending a pleasurable evening chatting with the other racers, had a good night's sleep. I was a wee bit nervous, but more than anything, I was excited.

The race started on Saturday at noon and went until Sunday at noon. The course began with a really steep rocky climb up the ski hills. When you got up to the top of that hill, you could see a sea of little tents at ground level below you. From the top of the hill, we rode into the woods. From there, the course flattened out and then it was all about a section of really hairy descending. In the middle of the descent, we went through a steep rocky area that people began to refer to as the "Bing Bang" because you'd go through it and get all binged and banged. When I got to the Bing Bang on my first lap around, I wondered how I would be able to get through that area in the middle of the night, but I had my lights charging down in the pit, and I figured I'd worry about that come nightfall.

From daylight to sunset, I did all right. I was surprised by how good I felt, considering I'd done so many laps of this wild course. Every time I made it to the pit, I'd grab a bottle, hydrate, and move on. If I got hungry, I'd grab something out of my bag and eat it on the go.

As night descended, I stopped in the pit and strapped my lights and batteries to my bike. The racecourse was by then pretty chewed up after eight or nine hours and countless laps. As I began to descend, there was a lot of dust, so much that it was reflecting off my lamp and making it difficult for me to see. It was scary, so I was on the brakes more and wasn't going too fast. I've always been a little cautious on descents, but with the dust blocking my sight, I was going pretty slowly.

After that first lap with my lamp, I started to notice that I couldn't see too well. By the time I got to the pit, I realized that my lights weren't working at all! I had an extra battery, so I plugged that in and went on, but halfway through the next lap, I realized that it wasn't working either! It was the rechargeable batteries I'd chosen: not a good strategy. I was out there with no batteries, no lights, and in total misery. I couldn't see a damn thing! I was also suffering from sleep deprivation and trying to force myself to stay focused, but my reflexes weren't at their best. The Bing Bang area was killing me. I crashed a half dozen times, and I was surprised I didn't total my bike.

Somewhere in the midst of all this, I decided that it would be a good time to crash for twenty minutes or so. I went out to the tents and asked a pit volunteer not to let me sleep for more than that. I didn't know how my body would react, if I'd even be able to get up afterwards, but I had to sleep. After about twenty minutes someone came and got me. I woke up right away and instantaneously felt alert. It was the strangest thing. That short rest pumped me full of energy. It only lasted another lap before I was sleepy again, but I knew that if I practised that skill I would be able to learn how to fight fatigue and sleep deprivation.

As insane as it was, I got through the night. As day started to break, my right hamstring and calf were cramping up like crazy. As I came down the mountain, I saw Nancy at a halfway point, near the pit. It was so cool to see her! She massaged my sore leg and cheered me on, and then a few other friends stopped in to give me some support. I might have been tired but that got me going again. It felt so good to see my friends!

I got back on my bike, with only one more lap to go. As I came through the finish line, I realized that at some point during the night, I had actually passed someone and had moved up to 2nd place! It was the first podium finish for me that didn't have anything to do with horses. I'd never thought that was even a possibility for me, especially with the way things had gone at the Quebec Cup. It felt amazing. I learned a valuable lesson. It was proof that working hard would land you a finish on the podium. I felt total personal satisfaction. Along with a finisher's medal, I also got a coffee mug, and I tell you, coffee out of that cup always tastes a little bit sweeter.

The rest of that year and into 2003 was a wild one for me. Following Bromont, I did a ton of stuff. I raced with Corey Gladish in the sea2summit Adventure Race, and also raced solo in the 24 Hours of Adrenaline in Massachusetts. In 2003, I entered the Eco-Challenge North American Championship with Beniot Letourneau and his team Simon River Sports, and then we did Raid the North shortly afterwards. Plus there was the TransRockies with Corey, a wild adventure that I'll never forget, mostly because I was out there with one of my best friends.

I had finally established in my mind that I really was an athlete. It was a crazy awesome year, but nothing could have prepared me for the day that I read about the Yukon Arctic Ultra in Dr. Smith's waiting room.

# CHAPTER TEN

Running for My Life
December 2003

By the time I left Dr. Duane Smith's office, the decision had been made. I would do it—I would run 160K in the Yukon. When I got home that afternoon, I called Pat, an adventure racer I'd met when I'd started working as a personal trainer. When he picked up the phone, I put it to him directly.

"Lookit. I'm going to do this running thing in the Yukon. The Yukon Arctic Ultra. Will you go running with me and show me how it's done?"

I don't remember if Pat laughed outright at the idea of me running 160K in below freezing temperatures, but I think he was amused. Either way, he agreed to help.

"No problem, man. I'll meet you at your place," he said.

True to form, Pat was up for a challenge. And I knew it would be a challenge!

Pat met me at my place in Chelsea. The man had a plan. We would chart a course along the main road, Highway 105, and make an 8K loop. It didn't seem like a lot, so I was confident about it. After all, I'd done all that mountain bike racing, and even some adventure races, and in one race, we'd trekked for 50K! I told myself that, but there was another voice inside me—one that reminded me how trekking for 50K was *very* different from running 160K consistently.

By this time in December, there wasn't actually that much snow on the ground, but it was very cold. We're talking long underwear under double-layered tights with an undershirt, T-shirt, sweatshirt, and a jacket and gloves!

Pat was jumping up and down to keep warm. He looked more than ready to go. All right, I told myself. Let's get this thing going.

"Okay, buddy," Pat said, jogging on the spot, "there's nothing to it. Just pick up one foot, put it in front of you, and put it down. Then repeat. And don't stop!" He loved to tease me.

We started off along the side of the highway, Pat to my side. I did what he told me and it seemed simple enough. I just picked up my foot and put it in front of me and then set it down. Easy enough, right? Those first 3K didn't seem too bad. In fact, I'd venture to say that they were a breeze. But then somewhere around 4K, that breezy feeling started to disappear and my breathing got heavier.

I looked over at Pat and noticed his smooth strides and easy inhalations. He was running at quite a clip. No sweat for Pat. He talked and tried to make conversation, but when he looked over at me and saw that I was beginning to struggle, he started to bark out orders.

"Watch your stride length!" he said.

"Breathe!"

"Stay relaxed!"

I tried to do what he said, but it was hard! By the time we got to about 6K, I had slowed down considerably. Man, is this ever tough, I thought. By 7K, I couldn't run anymore.

"Look man, I can't run. I gotta walk," I told Pat.

It was a full-body fatigue. My lungs weren't exactly burning, probably because of the cardiovascular strength I'd developed from mountain biking, but the pounding on the pavement killed my legs and feet, and my hips were really sore. We walked the rest of the way back to my place.

By the time we got home I'd caught my breath, but I was totally sore. I'd managed to run a total of 6K and walk another 2K. Not bad for a guy who'd never run before, but "not bad" wasn't going to get me through another 152K. I tried not to dwell on it.

And yet, I felt odd. *I felt like a runner.* Okay, I couldn't run very far and I couldn't run very fast, but I'd made a commitment and I had every intention of keeping it. I knew it was going to be tough: an awesome challenge. I knew the pain in my hips, back, feet, and legs was just the beginning. And I didn't care.

The next day, I called Brian and told him about my plans. Brian had always been athletic and he was totally into the idea of training with me. He had no intention of actually running the arctic himself, but he enjoyed pushing himself, a quality that always helps make a good athlete. In the weeks leading up to the race, he wouldn't act as my coach, but he was a good training partner and, as always, a good buddy. We decided we'd train together in the early morning hours on weekends. I was glad to have him out there with me, and I knew that just having him there was excellent motivation.

The day following that, I went out on my own and attempted the same 8K loop that Pat and I had done together. I was surprised to find that I didn't get winded as quickly and that I could complete the entire loop without having to walk. The day after that, I tacked on another 4K. Again, I managed it without having to walk. By my sixth run, I could already see a very marked improvement. I was going for longer and longer distances without getting winded. When I did get tired, I would stop running and start walking until I felt like I could start again. As my distances got longer, I had to stop and walk more and more often. But I felt focused, and seeing myself improve was hugely satisfying. It seemed simple: if I kept at it and stayed motivated, I *would* see an improvement. Not much in life is that simple, but running seemed so pure.

After that, I worked out a training schedule. On Mondays, Wednesday, Saturdays, and Sundays, I ran, and at least one of those runs would be an extra long one with Brian. Tuesdays and Thursdays I spun my legs on the bike.

By the beginning of January, I'd worked up to long distances in a short amount of time. At the time, 20 or 30K was a very, very long run for me. A run like that had me posted up on the couch for hours in searing pain. During those first few months of training, my body took some serious pounding. Sometimes I wondered why I was torturing myself, but other times the satisfaction of completing a goal made it all feel worthwhile.

On either Saturday or Sunday morning, Brian and I would go out for a really long run. We'd get up so early it was still dark out, and make our way out to the trails in the Gatineau Hills, along a totally awesome path that winds through Gatineau Park. We weren't really supposed to be there, since they were ski trails, and running through that new snow could make postholes and ruin the trail for the skiers. We didn't want to mess up their trails and also didn't want to run into any irate skiers, so we got up as early as possible and ran on the very edge of the trails. Sometimes Pat would join us and help out with tips. After a few weeks of training, when he reminded me to keep my breathing regular or to loosen up, I had a better understanding of what he meant. I learned early on how important it is to stay relaxed during a run.

After a couple of those longer runs, I decided that it was time to test out my stamina with the sled. I'd need to be dragging a sled throughout the entirety of the Yukon race. A backpack was out of the question; it would add way too much weight to the back and also cause serious post-holing.

The less weight on your back, the better. The sled had to house all your food and water and lots of mandatory emergency supplies. I needed to start thinking about that.

My landlord at the time was a guy named Richard Webber. Richard was the first guy to ski across the North Pole and I knew that he'd have some valuable information for me. I've always been an inquisitive person, but when I started running, I became doubly so. I wanted the advice of anyone who knew anything, and Richard Webber was no exception. I asked him what I would need to do to build a sled for the Arctic. At first he looked at me as though I were crazy, but I was getting used to that. Then he got down to it and showed me what I would need to do and explained some of the problems I would face—such as weight distribution, for instance. He made me think about the length of sled I'd need for the amount of gear I was bringing and how to pack that gear properly so that the weight would be properly distributed and the sled would slide with ease.

Richard gave me some great ideas and I thought about how I could customize what he had shared with me for my trip. The runners usually attached ropes to their sleds and pulled them, so I figured I could string those ropes through PVC piping and then attach them to my backpack using carabineers.

I checked out sled options on the Web and found all kinds of things. Some of the fancy sleds were upwards of a thousand dollars! But I didn't have that kind of money—nothing like it. I went to Wal-Mart and found a kid's sled for ten bucks. Sure, it was going to be pretty low-tech, but I figured that the sled wasn't as important as the motor pulling it.

I don't know what it was about the idea of running this race, or running at all, that got me so excited, but it had. The thrill of completing a goal, the peace and quiet I experienced during a run, even just looking down at my feet as they pounded the trail—everything about it just felt *right*. When I looked back at the last few years of my life, it seemed like everything had been leading up to this. I'd always hoped to find some passion in my life. Running filled that need. I felt like I was literally running for my life.

Towards the end of January, with less than three weeks to go before the race, I decided it was time to go out for a 60K—my first ever. I decided to bring the sled with me. I knew that during the race, our first mandatory checkpoint would be about four hours in, once we were nice and cold. That's when we'd have to show the crew that we were able to use all of our emergency gear. We'd have to light a fire, melt ice for water, and put up a tent. I wanted to make sure that I could do it, and I figured that I had an advantage since the weather in Ottawa was insanely cold already.

Brian came along. We started out early in the morning, before the sun was up. It was particularly cold that day. The winds were bitter too; it was like they were whipping my face. But I figured it was a good thing, to help give me a sense of how cold it would be out there in the Arctic. The truth is, I despise the cold. I mean, I'm a good Canadian, and I can handle some chilly weather, but -20°C is kind of nuts.

Brian and I ran for nearly ten hours that day, all through the snowy Gatineau trails. I don't remember what I was thinking. I just remember wanting to get through it, wanting to do the whole 60K with that sled behind me. All I remember was that by the time we were done, the sun was starting to set and that poor sled of mine was totally beaten up and bashed in. I'd torn the shit out of the bottom and it was completely ruined. I'd have to build a new one and I didn't mind a bit. I couldn't believe I'd run for 60K. It was amazing! I'd gone from not even being able to complete an

8K all the way to 60K, and I had the sore feet to prove it. That night, I dragged myself home feeling completely thrilled. And then I passed out on the coach.

That was the peak of my training. After that, I started to taper down and let my body recover. I used the last two weeks before the race to think about strategy and figure out exactly what I was going to bring with me. I needed a bivy sack (a basic portable shelter without any insulation), some ultra-warm but very light clothing, and a light tent. One of my clients, Mike Edelson, a man I'd been training for a while, asked me if I had any sponsors. Sponsors? I'd never thought of that. I told him I didn't.

"Well how are you going to get out there?" he asked me.

Again, I didn't know. Mike suggested that his law firm, Edelson & Associates, act as my first sponsor. I was stoked! Since then, Mike and I have become very good friends, and he was instrumental in getting me to all of my races. It would have been impossible without him. After that, Greg Christie, the owner of the bike store where I got my first bike, hooked me up with a bunch of warm lightweight clothing. My friend Dave Snow gave me a North Face suit. It was filled with down and incredibly warm. I felt very lucky to have such supportive friends.

I drew on the expertise of people I knew who had experience as runners, but I ultimately knew I was going to have to make the big decisions on my own. I tested my gear to make sure that I was proficient even in the worst weather, and I tested foods—mostly energy bars—to see which ones would hold out the best in the freezing temperatures. I wrapped my water bottles in closed-cell foam to try to keep the water from freezing. I tried out different layering systems with my clothing, made last minute arrangements, and booked time off from my clients.

There I was, two days before I was to leave for the race, a nervous wreck. Underneath all those plans and all that training, there was a huge amount of tension. I didn't feel prepared. I wasn't ready. I'd only done 60K, and I'd only done it once! Maybe I should have trained more, maybe I should've trained harder, maybe I hadn't trained right. There was that voice again, somewhere in the back of my head. Ray, it said, you have absolutely no idea what the hell you're getting yourself into.

Trying to stay warm during the four-hour mandatory stop at the Yukon Arctic Ultra, 2004

# CHAPTER ELEVEN

The Race of Discovery
February 2004

You can stumble around for your whole life, feeling like you don't know what you're doing and letting it get in your way or even letting it stop you. Or you can accept that maybe you don't know what you're doing but you're going to give it your best shot anyway. I adopted this latter attitude. I'll admit that it was often difficult to think that way. God knows I've had my share of anxiety and fear.

I loaded my cargo box—a huge gearbox covered with stickers and a big skull and crossbones I had drawn on it— onto the plane to Vancouver. From Vancouver, I caught a connected flight to Whitehorse International Airport in the Yukon. Sleepily, I dragged myself over to the luggage carousel to wait for my gearbox. The guy standing next to me was wearing a race T-shirt. I figured he was probably there for the same reason as me, but he looked nervous.

"I hope my luggage is okay," he said.

"Y'know," I said, "I'm sure it will be fine. I've never had any problem with my luggage before."

I could hear the crickets chirping. As soon as I said it, I knew something was going to go wrong. And wouldn't you know it, everybody else's stuff eventually came tumbling down that baggage carousel except for mine. I stood there feeling like a total idiot for saying that, as though I'd brought it on myself. On the other hand, how could they have lost the thing? It was an enormous Rubbermaid container, indestructible and highly visible.

What could I do? I knew there were going to be setbacks,

so I tried to take it in stride. The truth is I was pretty pumped about being there. I told myself to let it go and just go to the hotel. I didn't have any of my gear, but I wasn't going to let that stop me from running the race.

The first thing I noticed when I left the airport in Whitehorse was how much smaller the trees were than at home. I guess I had expected them to be enormous, but they looked like little brothers to the trees you might see in Ontario. There was a certain smell in the air that I noticed too. It was crisp and dry. The cold, too, seemed arid, much more dry than at home. Whitehorse appeared to be very spread out; there was an Old West Klondike feel to it that reminded me of old movies.

I boarded the shuttle bus that had been hired to take all the racers to the hotel and sat down next to a British couple. The woman turned to me.

"Are you the guy who lost his luggage?" she asked, by way of an introduction.

We introduced ourselves. Her name was Shirley Thompson, and her partner (and eventual husband) was named Mike Pemberton. Mike was a little frightening. He was extremely tall and very quiet, with eyes so piercing it felt like they were drilling holes into my skull. What I didn't know then was that they were both amazing runners and incredibly nice people. We'd eventually become good friends.

"So what races have you done before?" Shirley asked me.

"Uh, none," I told her. "I've done some adventure racing, but mostly mountain biking."

Her eyes got as big as silver dollars.

"What the hell are you doing here?" she asked me, shocked. "You're going to run for a hundred miles in the

Arctic?"

I laughed, thinking it did sound kind of wacky.

"Oh, what the hell," I told her. "I'm going to give it a try!"

They looked at me as though I were a complete nutter. Later, they admitted that they thought I didn't have a chance and that I would probably drop out entirely.

The atmosphere at the hotel was great. There were lots of runners milling about and meeting each other. A French runner named Jean-Michel introduced himself to me. We hit it off immediately. It was obvious we shared the same quirky sense of humour, and I could tell, almost by looking at him, that he was a good kind person. I also met Scotty Smith on that first night. The three of us became fast friends. When I was younger, I was intimidated by the idea of new situations, but the more I followed my heart and did the things I wanted to do, the more I enjoyed being in new situations and meeting new people.

The night before the event, we had a pre-race briefing. The race organizers went over the course with us and told us what to expect. I knew that I was over-prepared in terms of navigation. I had a GPS, and even topographical maps of the area. What did worry me, however, were some of the safety issues. Was I was prepared for frozen water or overflows? I wasn't keen on the idea of getting frostbite or, worse, hypothermia. But good news came when I found out that my gear had been located and would be flown in the next day, before the race started.

I didn't sleep all that well that night. I woke up feeling nervous and excited. Most of all, I just wanted to get started. I found Jean-Michel and Scotty, and together the three of us organized our gear and made our way to the start line. We were so busy joking around that I hardly had time to be nervous. On the way to the start line, we ran into another runner, a doctor from the United Kingdom. I'd met him the night before and had already taken to simply calling him Doc.

"Doc!" I called to him as we were approaching the race start line. "I'm in a lot of pain!"

"When does it hurt?" Doc asked me, without missing a beat.

"When I do this," I said and began to run.

Doc and Scotty laughed.

"Well," he said, in his a mock-serious doctor voice, "don't do that."

I was incredibly happy to see my gearbox when it finally made its way to the check-in. And yet, seeing my stuff again started to make me doubt my earlier choices. Seeing what the other runners were using, I felt slightly ashamed of my homemade Wal-Mart sled. I began to feel totally overwhelmed by the sheer distance of the race. Well, maybe I could just chew it off in small bites, I thought. But there was that voice again: Smaller bites? There are no *smaller* bites!

The Yukon Arctic Ultra had three different races that year: the regular marathon, a 160K, and a 300K. In the tradition of arctic racing that included three different disciplines—mountain biking, running, and skiing—they all have their advantages. Skiing on a frozen river can be very speedy, but when you get into the hills, a skier is going to be pretty limited. The same goes for mountain bikers; they can also go very fast on a frozen river. What can take a runner four or five hours, a skier or mountain biker can do in half the time.

The race was about to begin. We all assembled at the start. Quite a few people turned out to see us off at the beginning, mostly due to the fact that the Yukon Dog Quest was also happening in town and there were many people from all over the world who had come out to see that. Nevertheless, having people come out to the race was really cool. I looked around and felt good about what I saw: We were all there to challenge ourselves. I knew that I stood on the start line of something totally new for me, and I liked it. I didn't have any expectations beyond finishing the event, but I was determined to do that.

The race began with the sound of a starting pistol. I could feel the adrenaline as everyone started off in one big clump. It didn't take long before racers began to stagger and sort themselves out. We started off alongside the railroad tracks against the Yukon River. The first 40K would follow that same trail. The first checkpoint was the mandatory stop for the gear check. The organizers had planned it that way so that we'd already be cold and a little tired—a great time to check out gear and our ability to use it all. It would take four hours to go through it—the clock would stop and then start again when we were done. I tried to think of that first checkpoint as my goal. I told myself I would just run as fast and as far as I could. It was pretty much the only thought in my head: Just make it to the first checkpoint; just make it to the first checkpoint....

I felt pretty good during the first 40K, and they almost flew by without my noticing. I stayed relaxed and the constant movement kept me from getting cold. I was glad that I had prepared in the Gatineau trails, because I was accustomed to the snow and ice. I knew I had almost made it to the first checkpoint when I saw a steep hill ahead of me. I dragged my sled up the hill, and when I got to the top, I saw that a camp had been set up. That checkpoint was my first stop, but for some runners, it was the end of a marathon.

The large tent was set up with coffee and snacks. It wasn't warm by any means, but it was sheltered. A race volunteer greeted me and wrote down my number and time. There was only one other runner there, and a couple of skiers.

When I got into the checkpoint, I had no idea that Rob, the runner who had made it in before me, was in 1st place. My jaw nearly dropped when I discovered that I was actually in 2nd place! Things had gone well during the first 40K, but it hadn't occurred to me that I might be one of the front-runners. My mantra—just make it to the first checkpoint; just make it to the first checkpoint—had not only gotten me there, but had gotten me there in 2nd place! I was stoked.

The four hours at the checkpoint went by pretty quickly. It was probably from performing all those tasks. I unloaded the kit on my sled and demonstrated to the staff that I had everything on the gear list: my bivy sac, sleeping bag, medical kit, etc. I set up my tent and then hooked up my stove. This proved to be a tad more difficult than I had anticipated and I fumbled around in my gloves and mitts, attempting to light the stove and hook up the fuel canisters. I eventually got it working and I melted a bunch of snow in the pot to make drinking water.

As I was performing these tasks, some of the other runners began to catch up. I think a few runners were surprised to see me there, but everyone was really supportive. Runners congratulated me and told me how well I was doing. I was afraid that the other runners were just holding back because they knew I was inexperienced and foolish, and that they would suck me right back up in the middle of the night. I had to keep pushing.

Both Rob and I were done with our gear check around the same time, and we still had some time to spare, so we both busied ourselves repacking our sleds. I put everything back in carefully, making sure that I could access the things I thought I might need. I had overboots that would come in handy if I was confronted with a water crossing, so I put those on the top of my pack along with my water. When the four hours had passed, Rob and I were sent back out onto the trail. The sun was starting to go down. Rob and I took off together. We both wanted to get back down to the trail as quickly as possible to make use of whatever visibility was left.

We ran alongside the Yukon River for another 20K or so, and then left the frozen river to join what is referred to as the Braeburn Trail. There were indicators spray-painted into the snow—arrows that pointed us in the right direction—but they were sporadic and frankly, hard to find. Both Rob and I were nervous about going off track because in the darkness everything was beginning to look similar. We eventually made our way to the trail without too much difficulty.

It was good to be running with someone. It was nice to have another person out there with me, and we chatted as we ran. As the sun set, we pulled out our headlamps and strapped them to our heads. I had my first glimpse of the northern lights; it was like nothing else I'd ever seen before. It was like a curtain of fluorescent light across the sky—an amazing sight to behold.

By then, I had developed something of a technique. I'd noticed that to gain better traction, I had to take shorter strides and keep my upper body as relaxed as possible. I picked my way through the terrain and tried not to punch through the snow.

As we ran, I tried to remember to keep hydrated, but I really wasn't drinking as much water as I should have. I had two large plastic drinking bottles with me, the ones I had wrapped in closed-cell foam to keep the water from freezing.

It's the same kind of foam you might use underneath a sleeping bag. I'd duct-taped it around the bottles. That didn't add any weight to them at all, which was good, but even after all that, I still wasn't drinking enough water. I was dehydrated. I'd stopped at the side of the trail before the first checkpoint to pee and I hadn't felt the need to go since. I knew that that kind of dehydration could cause a serious problem, so I tried to make up for it by eating as much snow as possible. I noticed that Rob wasn't eating or drinking at all, and that also concerned me.

I don't know how many kilometres we had covered on the Braeburn trail before I started to notice that Rob was beginning to slow down. Before long, he started to look pretty bad, and he was running in something of a weaving motion. I ran along with him like that for a while, but I knew that he hadn't eaten enough and I had to say something.

"Okay, man, when was the last time you ate?" I asked him.

Rob waved it off. A lot of ultramarathoners are hard as nails, and Rob's no exception. He said he was all right, so we kept going at a slower pace. It wasn't long before he stopped running and began to walk. It wasn't long before I started to get cold as my body temperature dropped.

I asked him again when he had last eaten. Rob explained that hadn't really been able to eat. He felt nauseated. I pulled some of the energy bars out of my bag and gave them to him.

"Dude," I said, "you've gotta eat."

Rob took the bars and ate as much as he could. By now, we were walking and I was getting really cold. I knew there was safety along the course: staff on Ski-Doos going up and down the trails every now and then to make sure everything was okay. Rob was a very experienced runner, and being from Whitehorse himself, he knew the lay of the land. I also knew that if I didn't start running again, I'd go hypothermic. I think Rob could tell, too, because he insisted that I start running again. I told him I'd run out to the next checkpoint and get help, but he assured me that he was fine. Eventually, I started running again, this time alone.


There was a checkpoint about 20K away. I was dangerously cold and although I knew I was now in 1st place, I didn't have the peace of mind to be excited about it—I was too concerned about Rob. I focused my mind on getting to the next checkpoint so that I could tell staff that Rob was back there and could use encouragement.

I ran towards that checkpoint as fast as I could but the Braeburn Trail was starting to get hilly and I was feeling pretty tired. Actually, I was exhausted. It was very dark out there. My mind started to play tricks on me. I started to see stairs (staircases!) in the middle of the forest. Every sound I heard freaked me out; just the regular sounds of the forest— snow falling from a tree, the rustling of the branches in the wind—started to sound really creepy. That's what happens when exhaustion sets in: you can get paranoid. Even worse, I started to fall asleep as I was running. I knew I had to stop.

I took my ski poles that I had been using to help me on the hills and pointed them in the direction I was headed so that when I woke up, I would know which way to go. I pulled out my bivy sack and opened it up. I threw it on the ground and got in, with my headlamp and all, and set my watch alarm for exactly two minutes. I fell asleep in a heartbeat.

*Beep! Beep! Beep!*

My watch went off. I woke up and put my things away. Amazingly, those two minutes really made a difference. It was enough recovery for me to keep going. I felt a million times better.

When I got to the checkpoint, I told them about Rob. I was very relieved to hear that someone had spotted him on the trail and he was just fine.

Meanwhile, the staffers at the checkpoint were surprised. They were pretty shocked at how fast I had arrived there, and when I found out, so was I. There were other skiers there, but I was the first runner. This was something else! The skiers had the upper hand when it came to crossing flat terrain. I didn't understand how I could have caught up with them. What was even more amazing was that they told me I was on pace to best last year's winning time. I just couldn't believe it. I was beyond exhilarated.

Back then, I didn't know that I had the ability to run long distances. All I knew was that I wanted to complete the race. Until that point, that had been my only motivation. In many ways, I think my *lack* of expectation was exactly what allowed me to do so well. I connect it to the way my parents brought me up. What I think I mean is that since I didn't have any particular expectations on my race time, anything was possible. When you believe you can only run so fast, or for so long, you're actually limiting yourself.

For the first time in my life, I was in 1$^{st}$ place. I wanted it to stay that way. Was I focused? If I hadn't been before, I was then. I left that checkpoint with a mental stubbornness that carried me through the dawn and into early morning. Did my feet hurt like hell? They did. Was I exhausted? I was. But after learning I was in 1$^{st}$ place and had a shot at winning the race, I left with as light a step as possible under the gruelling circumstances.

Although I am ultimately an extrovert, I do like to be alone during races. I'm very comfortable with that solitude and I think it's good for me. All the sounds of daily life—television, radio, car horn, people talking and yelling and laughing—are forgotten during a race. It's good to spend time with yourself, checking in with your own feelings and simply allowing your brain to wander wherever it likes.

As I ran along the trail, a million thoughts drifted through my mind. I counted down the kilometres as I went and dreamed of getting to the lodge, taking off all my racing gear, putting my feet up, and eating to my heart's content. Although I allowed my mind to wander, I also made sure that I was in charge of it too. I had to stay focused, so I'd reel my thoughts back to the race. Still, I have to admit that there were hours that simply went by unaccounted for, when I was literally thinking of nothing at all.

It was daybreak when I noticed a small tent set up on the side of the trail. A cross-country skier named Laszlo, whom I had met at the hotel stuck his head out and yelled out to me.

"Ray!" he yelled, in his thick Hungarian accent. "Ray, you are crazy!"

I laughed, thinking maybe he was right, and kept going.

A checkpoint appeared in the distance. It was the third and last before the lodge and the end of the race. In the distance, I thought I could make out skiers, but I figured I was probably just hallucinating. When I got in, however, I saw that there were, in fact, skiers. I couldn't believe it! How had I caught up to them? I didn't even want to stop except to fill up my water bottles. I thought that if I sat down, my feet would turn to brick and my hips would go to jelly. I certainly thought I wouldn't be able to get back up, so I kept on, one step at a time, and did my best to maintain focus.

The going got rough though. I was dangerously dehydrated and still hadn't peed since that first break early on. I knew that was no good. Although my two-minute catnap had helped, I was feeling the effects of sleep deprivation. I kept going, since that was the only course of action I was prepared to take.

Somewhere around 130K, I saw a couple of guys on a Ski-Doo approaching me. One of them was a reporter from Europe and had a video camera with him. He asked me how I was doing. I don't remember what I said, but I remember thinking: I'm exhausted, I feel like a bag of shit, my feet are killing me, and I'm dehydrated. However, I think my actual response was something more along the lines of: "I feel great!"

The reporter asked me when I expected to be done. I did the calculations in my head. I had about 30K more to go and I was running about 6K an hour. I figured it would take me another five hours if all went well—the snow was deep.

"So, cheers, guys!" I yelled out, as I turned to get back to the trail.

My body was just about broken by then. Everything was so sore, from my feet to my head. I didn't want to take any ibuprofen, because I was already too dehydrated. The water in my bottles had frozen over by then, so I had no other choice but to grab handfuls of snow and shove them into my mouth. Fortunately, there was no lack of snow! I laughed when I thought about the old adage: Never eat yellow snow. It was actually applicable in my case, what with the dogsledders so nearby.

The trail was beginning to get really hilly, and my glutes and hamstrings were in knots. The pain was so bad I wanted to scream.

I was only 10K from the finish line when the voice inside my head started to get progressively louder: This is too much, it's too hard, you need to sit down. Every couple of paces, I had to stop and squat on the ground. It eventually got to be that I would stay down for two or three minutes and then have to will myself back up again. I'd covered so much ground and only had a short distance to go, but it seemed insurmountable. I stopped running and began to walk. Then I saw a lake. I knew all I had to do was cross the lake and I would see the lodge. I picked up my pace. The voice was still there, but with a different message: You can do this; you can finish. But I knew I just had to get across the lake.

When I got across the lake, I remembered what someone had told me the night before: Don't be fooled when you see the lodge, because once you get there, even though there's only a few more kilometres to go, you're still going to have to go up and down a series of short steep hills.

It was true. It was everything I'd heard and worse. My sled kept getting stuck and I got frustrated. After having covered over 157K of tough snow-covered terrain, I suddenly felt my will power give out. Poof. I sat down on my sled and gave in. I was thirsty, I was tired, and it was just too hard. I wanted to cry. The voice in my head was telling me to lie down. And why not? I *was* very tired. Why shouldn't I lie down and close my eyes? It would feel so nice to just sleep…just for a minute….

I nearly did give up. It would have been quite easy to stop. But I was so close to the finish and I had made a promise to myself. The commitment that I had made to finish this race had been an important one for me. I knew that it wasn't going to be easy. But did I even want it to be? What was *easy*? Easy meant quitting, it meant giving up. I didn't want to do those things. I wanted to finish. I wanted to silence that negative voice that told me I couldn't do the things I set out to do. I stood up and I went for it.

Those last 3K hurt like hell. They were by far the

toughest in the race, but I kept going. After each agonizing step, I got closer to the lodge. And then, miraculously, I was there, at the lodge, and I crossed the finish line.

But there was nobody there! Not a soul. I walked into the lodge and poked my head in. I saw several organizers and staff members inside.

"Hey, guys!" I said. "I'm done."

Heads turned.

"What?"

"Huh?"

"You're here? Already?"

"What the—?"

At first I thought they were pulling my leg. Maybe the exhaustion was messing with my head, but I didn't see what all the fuss was about. They told me I'd topped last year's time for the 160K! I was floored! I didn't think I'd done anything out of the ordinary—I'd only been trying to get it done! I was so happy that I wanted to dance, except that my feet hurt too much.

I knew when I closed me eyes and slept, I'd be out for a very long time, so I wanted to make sure I didn't go to bed on an empty stomach. I sat my sore body down and ate everything that looked good, which was just about everything. I pigged out on the world's biggest hamburger and washed it down with the world's biggest cinnamon bun—the lodge's specialties. As the pain really began to sink in, so did the bliss. I was ecstatic. I felt like I had finally found the answer to a question I'd always wanted to know.

# CHAPTER TWELVE

The Itch
March 2004

Life changed for me after the Yukon Arctic Ultra. Winning the race was a complete shock to my system. I felt great about it, but what felt even better was the sensation that for the first time in my life, I had found something that I was truly passionate about. There was no doubt about it: Ultrarunning was what I wanted to do. I had direction and goals I truly cared about. When people asked me what I did, I said it with pride: I'm a runner. I was proud to be the person I was.

That said, when I got home from the race, I was in a whole lot of pain. It took me over two weeks to recover, and my feet were the worst part of it. They weren't used to covering that kind of distance back then. By definition, I could *walk*, but it was a pretty funny version of walking: the arches of my feet were so sore that I couldn't walk on them, so I had to walk on my heels. It didn't matter though. A pair of sore feet was par for the course. I was an ultrarunner, and the pain was part of the job.

But there was one exception to the pain I experienced: my back. During the race, I'd expected it to go at any minute. When I got home and it still didn't feel sore, I could hardly believe it. The fear of upsetting my condition had always been in the back of my mind. Knowing it could flare up unexpectedly, and that I would go through a cycle of pain for several weeks before it healed again, had always been a huge barrier for me. It was always in the way. I don't know why my back didn't hurt. After a race like that, it should have. All I know is that it didn't, and that helped me break through the fear. I became more confident in my body than ever before.

Everyone back home was psyched that I had won. John, Brian, Pat, Greg Christie, Dave Snow, and Mike Edelson had all been on board since the very beginning, so seeing me win my first race was awesome. My clients, who had all been extremely supportive from the get-go, were all happy for me when I told them the news. My parents were pleased too, but I got the sense that they weren't entirely buying the idea that I would commit myself to running forever. I think they wondered if I was experiencing an early mid-life crisis. Nevertheless, they saw that I had made some major changes in my life, and they both respected that.

During the two weeks that I hobbled around in pain, I also made a formal commitment to run the Marathon des Sables in Morocco. I had pre-entered the race before even going to the Yukon, mainly because Pat was doing it, but back then it had seemed like a reach. That changed when I got back from the Yukon. I had the itch! Marathon des Sables was a stage race, meaning the runners cover 243K over a period of six days. Plus it was in Morocco! It sounded like too much fun to pass up.


I didn't have much of a social life in those days. By then, a lot of my friends had moved away or gotten married. I didn't have much time to socialize anyway. When I wasn't working with my clients, I was training. I worked my ass off during the week and took on as many clients as I could handle. I needed to save up enough money to get to Marathon des Sables. It wasn't going to be cheap.

There were some people who thought I was crazy, and others who thought I was an addict; that I'd just replaced alcohol with running. Sometimes people would ask me questions such as: "What are you running from?"—a question I've always gotten a kick out of. I never took it to heart because I understood why they thought what they did. Hey, my first reaction to the Yukon Arctic Ultra was similar. But the thing is, it also made sense to me. It didn't take more than a couple of seconds after seeing that magazine article before I was hooked. Right away, I saw the sport as something that was challenging in every way. It appealed to me, plain and simple, and I never felt the need to justify that.

As far as running being an addiction, well, who knows? Maybe it is. I love running. I think about it all the time. I love pushing myself to the limit and seeing what my body can do. If I've had a stressful day, I almost always turn to running to relieve some of that stress. So I think it's fair to say there's a need for it. If for some reason I couldn't run anymore, I probably *would* turn to another sport. Maybe I'd go back to mountain biking, or perhaps I'd find something new. But I don't think that the passion would be there. I know that there are runners out there who are faster than me, but I really don't care. I just love to do it. So if that's an addiction, fine by me. Besides, I'd much rather be addicted to something that keeps me physically fit and mentally sharp than be addicted to something like cigarettes, which put me at risk for cancer, numbs my taste buds, and costs me a ton of money, or alcohol, which keeps me apathetic and depressed. Give me a run over a smoke and a drink any day.

But I'm not a complete lunatic. I spent two weeks recuperating after the Yukon, and I'm proud to say I didn't go for one run during that time. Instead, while I was posted up, I started poking around at my gear, trying to figure out what I would need for the Marathon des Sables. I wouldn't need a sled, but I would need a pack, and it would have to contain my food, clothing, sleeping bag, hydration system, medical gear, and whatever else I'd need for a six-day jog across the Sahara Desert. Plus, it would be much heavier than anything I was accustomed to.

I put a lot of thought into my pack and how to keep it as light as possible. Anything you take to the race has to stay with you the whole time. It is absolutely forbidden to jettison anything that proves to be too heavy in the desert, so I wanted to make sure I had it right.

Pat had competed in the race the year before. He told me as much as he could about it. He described the sandstorms, the deep sands, and the heat. He actually managed to freak me out a bit. I didn't know whether he was exaggerating, and I was so brand new to the world of ultramarathons that I took everything he said very seriously. I wanted to be prepared.

I got to thinking about the sand and the heat. I figured that the best way to keep the sun off my legs and the sand out of my pants was to wear long running tights. I packed two extra pairs of socks, plus the ones I planned to wear. I picked up a buff, a multi-functional tube of material like a bandana that can be worn on the head in a variety of ways, which I planned to use to keep the sun off my head during the day. I bought a heavy toque for the nights, and then packed a variety of extra clothes.

I then devised a lightweight system for my food. I bought dehydrated foods as high in calories as I could find. I found a particular brand of dehydrated chicken gumbo that was extremely high in calories, and picked up as many of those as I thought I could eat, which was a lot. Then I removed all the dried foods from their original packaging and transferred them into Ziploc bags. Doing that saved me several grams per package, and when you add up a week's worth of food, it actually shaved off lots of packaging weight. I purchased a very lightweight stove too. It was small enough to fit in my pack. It was made of tin and had small solid fuel cubes inside it. The fuel weighed a bit more than I would have liked, but I needed to be able to use the stove.

The final consideration was my shoes. I was worried about the sand getting into them, but I didn't know how to keep it out. I finally settled on a system that I thought was pretty ingenious: I simply wrapped my shoes with duct tape from top to bottom, using glue to be sure it would stay in place. All in all, my pack weighed about twenty-three pounds. I figured I could manage that.

When I was finally able to start training again, I knew there were things that I wanted to change and improve. Training for the Yukon had been pretty simple: I was just getting used to running, period. But Marathon des Sable was different. It was a stage race, for one thing, and for another, it was all about speed. So I redesigned my training program to include more speed work. I also started running with a loaded pack. It wasn't exactly winter anymore, but spring in the Ottawa Valley can be pretty snowy nonetheless, and I was still running on leftover slush, muck, and snow on the trails.

During the weekdays, I concentrated on getting faster. I did a lot of tempo runs. I warmed up for ten minutes, ran 5K as fast as I could, slowed down for another 5K, then sped up again, and so on, over and over. I also did kilometre repeats: I ran as hard as I could for 1K and recorded my time. Then I took a few minutes to cool off and went at it again. On the weekends, I did long distances by going for 40K at a time. Plus, I stepped up the number of days I ran from four to five a week.

I also drank a lot of water while I was training. I wasn't going to run the risk of getting dehydrated again, especially in the heat of the desert. I vowed to keep myself hydrated. I figured out a system that I thought would work well. I knew a lot of people would be using hydration bladders—those plastic bags that sit in your backpack with tubes that act as straws. I figured those weren't a good idea for me. For one thing, I didn't want to use the same bag for water as I used for Gatorade or hydration formula. Another thing was the nozzle: In the middle of the desert, I could imagine it touching all kinds of things and getting very dirty, possibly making me sick. Instead, I just chose to bring two bottles and sanitizer to keep them as clean as possible.

The idea was to try to recreate the stages I'd be dealing with in the race. That was my main concern. When I had trained for the Yukon, I'd only run four times a week, one day on and one day off, giving my body a day to recover. But for this race, I ran five days a week straight. The race would be six days and that made me nervous. I didn't want my body to seize up when I stopped for the night—a legitimate concern.

Another thing that made me edgy was the idea of sleeping on the ground in tents. I figured that after a long day of hard running, sleeping on the ground was going to be tough, not to mention the fact that since we were expected to bring along all our own foods, and carry it, I probably wouldn't be nourishing myself properly. It's not like I'd be able to run around the desert with a piece of grilled chicken in my pack, if you know what I mean.

After nearly a month and a half of training, it was time to go. Pat was signed up for the race as well, but he wasn't in Ottawa, so he told me to bring his gear along and that he'd meet me in Morocco. Brian dropped me off at the airport in Montreal, where all the Canadian runners were to meet.

That was my first introduction to a handful of people who are now good friends of mine. The first person I met in the airport was Ken Davis. We hit it off immediately. Ken would've been in his late forties then. He had a silly sense of humour that always cracked me up. He was from Toronto and was going to be doing the race for the second time. He and I hung out in the Royal Air Maroc waiting area, waiting for the rest of the Canadian runners to show up.

Slowly but surely, everyone came. There was Mark and his wife, Joanie, and Sue and Sandy, among others. We were all ready to get on that plane, but we instead ended up sitting on the floor as long lines began to snake around the airport. There was some kind of delay and we were all feeling it. The upshot was that waiting on that delay gave us all a chance to get to know each other. We sat around and talked about our gear and the race, and my impression was that I was hanging out with a pretty cool crowd of people. Mark in particular was very knowledgeable and I knew that he and his wife would have a lot of valuable information to share with me. In fact, Mark ended up with the nickname Big Brother because I asked him so many questions.

I was incredibly psyched to get to Morocco. The furthest away I'd ever been was Scotland, and the idea of going to Africa was totally incredible to me.

When we got to Casablanca, we didn't even leave the airport, but I was still excited. I kept thinking: I'm in Africa...I'm in Africa! As we walked past a bookshop in the airport, I saw a book about the Sahara that had big gorgeous pictures of the sand dunes. I couldn't wait to see them in real life. As beautiful as any photograph can be, it can't ever compare to the real thing.

The airport in Casablanca was quiet that day. Going through customs was a snap. The only unusual thing I noticed about the airport was that people were smoking inside. Also, rather than the drab colours you usually see in airports, Casablanca had beautiful marble floors and mosaics on the walls. The space was much more interesting and artistic than any airport I'd ever been to.

The Canadian runners and a handful of tourists (there were maybe nine of us) boarded a small prop plane from Casablanca to Ouarzazate, where we would be staying for a couple of nights before getting bused out to the desert. Ouarzazate is a quiet town in the south of Morocco. As we flew south from Casablanca, I had my nose glued to the window the whole time, hoping to catch a glimpse of the dunes. Instead, I saw a lot of open barren land. That just served to pique my interest even more. I thought about my dad and wondered whether Morocco was anything like Lebanon. For some reason, I felt like it was. I wished he could be out there with me, participating in the race. Before his stroke, he'd always been in excellent shape.

Our plane landed on a small strip at Ouarzazate Airport. We exited the plane in the middle of the landing strip, and as I made my way down the airplane's stairs, the heat hit me like a ton of bricks. It was the very beginning of April and it felt like a million degrees out there. The smell reminded me of summertime in Canada, but it was also sweet and thick and rich. I was blown away. It was unusual and yet, for some reason, it seemed vaguely familiar. I've only ever smelled that scent in Africa, and whatever it is, I love it.

The airport was a few hundred yards away—a small, almost cute, terracotta-coloured concrete structure. There were security guards to guide us through the check-in, and tall palm trees swaying in the hot breeze.

The sensations of that air on my skin, the sun beating down on me, and that foreign yet familiar smell were all very appealing to me. I felt a strange connection with the climate. I knew then that the desert was the place for me. I knew I would be back.

# CHAPTER THIRTEEN

The Race of Mistakes
April 2004

We all got into taxis and barrelled off onto the highway towards downtown Ouarzazate. Even the ride into town was exciting; taxis and cars alike weaved in and out of traffic as though they were racing. When we got into the village, I saw that the architecture looked vaguely European in some parts, yet it was different from anything I had ever seen.

I learned that Ouarzazate also hosted film sets on the outskirts of town. *Sodom and Gomorrah*, and later *Kingdom of Heaven* and *Babel* were shot there. It was amazing to think of the cultural contrasts. I tried to imagine Ouarzazate in its heyday, when they shot *Lawrence of Arabia* there. It seemed so magical. Some of the hotels on the main street appeared to have been built back then too. They were grand structures.

Our hotel was beautiful too. The floors and ceilings were covered in mosaics. I was so impressed that I asked one of the hotel employees how the mosaics had been installed. He told me that someone in town had painstakingly painted and cut each and every piece. I was in awe at that kind of attention to detail and care.

After dropping our things off in our rooms, we decided to do some exploring. We walked over to the main street. The street was chock full of little cafés and restaurants and tiny stores with men standing outside beckoning for us to come inside.

"Come in, come in!" they'd yell to us. "We have specials for you!"

Between the shop owners and the café-goers, there was certainly a lot of action in the streets. As we were walking along, poking our heads into this and that little store, one shop caught my eye. Like all the others, it was no more than a tiny hole in the wall, but there were so many strange and interesting things sitting out there. I saw some old equestrian equipment and a pair of wooden doors. I was very intrigued, so I popped my head into the darkness of the shop. I saw a middle-aged man with a pair of bright honest eyes staring back at me. I saw that there were two young men at the back of the store, too. We exchanged greetings and he invited me in.

The store was like a very narrow hallway full of ancient relics. It was smoky and dark inside, and smelled strongly of incense. The walls were covered in tattered rugs and old paintings. Everything you could ever imagine was there in that store somewhere: slippers, ashtrays, leather bags, jewellery.

The older man introduced himself and told me that the boys in the back were his two sons. Mr. Ahmed invited me to sit down and have a cup of mint tea with him. It was an incredibly sweet concoction of sugar and mint leaves crushed up at the bottom of the glass. It was delicious. After we finished our tea, Mr. Ahmed told me he had something for me. I told him that I hadn't brought much money with me, but that I did have an extra pair of running shoes in my bag. They were brand new and I didn't need them for the race.

"Okay," Mr. Ahmed said, "I'll trade you. My son could use a pair of shoes."

He handed me a strange silver ornament attached to a leather necklace and told me it was the Cross of Agadez, a symbol of the Touareg culture. He told me that it symbolized the cross of the south. I thought it was very beautiful. I accepted it with great thanks and put it around my neck.

Stepping off the plane in Morocco with my fellow Canadian racers

Ready, set, go! Marathon des Sables, 2004

I've seen many of these silver crosses since. They're something that tourists often buy, and there are over fifty different types of crosses. But the one Mr. Ahmed gave me was special. I've never seen one like it, and to this day, I'm sure mine is special. The Touareg people aren't Moroccan, they're a nomadic people from the Sahara, and the cross of Agadez comes from Niger. I didn't know then that nearly a year later, I'd be running across Niger. I wear the necklace that Mr. Ahmed gave me to this very day.

Back at the hotel, I enquired as to whether anyone had heard from Pat, but there was no sign of him. As I was stood there, I saw a blond woman and a man with glasses. The woman looked familiar, so I asked about her. I was told it was Lisa Smith-Batchen and her husband, Jay. I had read all about Lisa since returning from the Yukon. She was an amazing runner. I was really excited to meet her and her husband and they were both exceptionally nice people. After we chatted for a bit, I went to my room and began to go through my gear. I had brought more than I needed with me and wanted to whittle it down to the bare essentials.

Once all the racers had made it to town, it was time to get out into the desert. I threw my pack on and, along with the rest of the racers and crew, boarded one of the large shuttle buses. I kept waiting for the scrub and rocks to give way to sand, but I was out of luck. We drove over a mountain pass. I noticed that there were no guardrails. Our bus was speeding down the road and I was freaked! After several hours of driving on paved roads, we broke off onto gravel. Still no sand. After a few more hours, we went off-road completely. The bus, although large and steady, drove at quite a clip. It seemed to sway back and forth. Finally, after nearly seven hours, the buses stopped. They could go no further. We piled out and saw that there were huge dump trucks waiting to take us into the camp.

When we got to our camp, I saw over eighty large Berber tents set up in the flat rocky field. The shelters looked like they were made out of massive coffee bags. They were black burlap held up with wooden poles. The tents had about six inches of clearance along the bottom to let air in, but in a sandstorm, you could protect yourself by pulling the tent down and weighing the sides down with rocks. I was exhausted from the long trip into the desert. I walked to the Canadian tents, which were set about a mile back from the race start line. I unpacked my gear, unrolled my sleeping pad, and then went out to meet with the other racers for the dinner that Marathon des Sables had prepared for us. It would be our last real meal before we had to fend for ourselves.

Out in the middle of the desert sat a huge truck with big balloon tires. It was enormous—almost as big as an eighteen-wheeler. The sides of the truck opened up to reveal that it was modified to cater a crowd. There was a long line snaking all the way around the truck, but it was well worth the wait. There was a complete buffet offered: a French meal consisting of pasta, baguettes, soup, salad, and little bottles of red wine for anyone who wanted one. The food was amazing. As I sat on a rock, eating my last real dinner and chatting with other racers, I noticed that since the sun had set, the temperature had dropped considerably. It was actually almost cold.

I woke up the next morning as stiff as a board. The sleeping pad I had brought was not doing the trick. For all the good it did me I may as well not have brought anything at all. My hips were killing me. Mistake number one, I thought. Oh well.

It was gear-check day, and Pat still hadn't made it. I

knew then that he wasn't coming. I was pretty disappointed. I had been looking forward to hanging out with him, and I felt I needed his expertise. I didn't know anything about going out into the desert on my own!

I went through my gear for the last time and figured out once and for all what I was bringing with me. My pack still weighed about twenty-three pounds. I divvied up the food from Pat's pack amongst anyone who need it, and tossed the bag. You can't bring anything into the desert that you don't plan on keeping with you the whole time, so I had to let it go. Then I went through gear check. I was a little nervous—missing mandatory gear can get you a time penalty—but I had everything.

That night, my nerves kicked in. I calmed myself by thinking about all the preparation I had put into this race. The next morning, I woke to the sound of trucks as the Berber crews took the tents down. They were in such a serious hurry that if you didn't get your things together in time, you could end up being carted off with the tents. They had to get out to the next site and put the camps back up, so they were in a rush.

The camp was full of action. There was loud rock music blaring from the speakers and announcements on the microphone. The race director was on top of his Land Cruiser, shouting out instructions. All the runners—there were nearly 750 of us, from all sorts of different countries—were milling about, preparing to run. Everyone was instructed to gather round. Before the race began, we all took a picture of ourselves in the formation of the number 19 to commemorate the nineteenth year of the Marathon des Sables. The next year would be the 20th anniversary, and that one was sure to be spectacular.

The next thing I knew, the countdown began. The first

leg of the race was only 28K. I had butterflies in my stomach, but I was excited. The gun went off, and I took off running. It was an amazing feeling. I felt so good in the desert. I knew that every step I took was getting me closer to the sand dunes. As I ran, I congratulated myself on my shoe system. My pack felt good too. What I didn't understand yet was that stage races are tough in a different way, since your body never really has a chance to recover.

When I got to the first checkpoint and received my two rations of water, I had to stop to transfer the water from the bottles they had given me into my own. I quickly realized that I had made a mistake that would cost me time: Instead of just taking the bottles they handed off, I had to stop and do the switch. A few minutes here and a few minutes there quickly added up. But I didn't do too badly in that first day; I think I finished somewhere in the top 30.

At camp that night, I went through the series of activities I would do every night for the next five: I stopped and stretched, unloaded my gear, and then made something to eat—usually the dehydrated chicken gumbo I'd brought so much of. I noticed that there weren't very many runners with little stoves like mine, and I wondered about it until I saw what everyone else was doing: they were simply mixing their dehydrated food with lukewarm water in a bag and then letting it sit out in the sun long enough to heat up. I realized I had made another major mistake: I didn't need my whole stove and fuel system. No matter how light it was, it was unnecessary. I wished I could dump it, but that was out of the question. Oh well, I thought as I heated up my gumbo. I was just happy to have something to eat.

I woke up the morning of day two stiffer than ever. My hips were really killing me, and now my back was starting to hurt. I cursed my sleeping pad as the Berbers tore down the tents as fast as can be. The course on day two was 34K. When we started out, there was still a lot of gravel and stone on the desert floor, but as we went further along the course, the shrub and trees disappeared and gave way to light sand. It looked to me like a beach that never ended. I saw my first glimpse of the dunes that day. They were just dunettes, tiny versions of what I would see later, but I was still so excited. It was the highlight of my whole day. I noticed about halfway through the day that I had been running next to the same guy for quite a while, so I introduced myself. His name was Gavin, a British runner. In a long race like that, you make friends quickly. We got to talking and decided that we would run together.

That night, everyone was talking about how important your standing on day three would be. Day four was the really long day: 76K. Whereas everyone usually started at the same time, that would change for day four. There were two start times: one in the morning and one at noon. The top 50 runners would start later, and the other 700 runners would go out earlier in the morning. There were advantages to both. Obviously, being in the top 50 was great, since it meant you were doing really well, but it would also mean that you would have to run on sand that had already been chewed up by 700 other runners. To make things worse, you'd have to sit around camp half the day in the sweltering heat. Starting in the morning meant that you had a chance of finishing the course before dark. Everyone had a different theory about which was better. I didn't know what to do, so I decided to just let fate take its course. I'd run and see what happened.

Gavin and I ran together during stage three. We were working together really well, and it was fun to have someone there to chat with. The course was 37K that day. Within the first 15K, I could see the dunes off in the distance: they were

Berber tents in Morocco

Treating blisters in
between stages –
Marathon des Sables,
2004

great mountains of sand. I couldn't wait to get close to them, but my motor just wasn't running as fast as I would have liked it. Gavin and I ran and then walked, ran then walked. Even the promise of getting close to the dunes couldn't make me go any faster.

We finally got to the dunes. They were massive! When we got to the top of the first dune, I looked around. All I could see beyond me was more dunes. I had no idea how far the desert could stretch out. It was just sand everywhere, sand and sky. I was so happy…until I looked down at my feet.

I noticed that the duct tape on my shoes had completely peeled away. The fine grains of sand had got underneath the tape and destroyed the adhesive. The sand was pouring into my shoes like icing sugar through a sieve. I'd thought my whole shoe system was so brilliant, but instead it was kicking my ass. I knew that my feet would be totally blistered by the end of the day.

The dunes were gorgeous, but they were incredibly hot too. My long running tights started to feel oppressive and I could feel that the chaffing on my back would give way to blisters too. I looked down and saw an Italian runner at the bottom of a dune. He had kicked his shoes off and was running through the sand with bare feet, talking to himself and cackling the whole time. It looked like he had gone crazy, like the desert had driven him mad. Maybe that's what the Marathon des Sable is: a place for us crazies. Still, I was happy to be there. As I stood at the top of that first dune and surveyed the great wide desert before me, I remembered the day I had first climbed those mountains with John. It didn't matter that everything was falling apart. I felt like I'd arrived.

I limped into the finish at the end of stage three with blisters all over my feet and back. They needed to be drained and taped. I stretched and then started making myself something to eat: another pack of dried gumbo. It seemed like it was the only thing any of the North American runners were eating. Kenny in particular was so sick of it that he actually starting puking. He just couldn't take it anymore.

The worst part about the gumbo fiasco is that the packaging had fooled us all. The printed label said it had a super high calorie count, but when I did the math myself, I realized it was a misprint. Yet another mistake! The mistakes seemed to be piling up: my shoes, my tights, my sleeping pad, my stove, the weight of my pack, my water system, my food! Everything! It bothered me, but I also knew that I was learning valuable lessons. I wouldn't make the same mistakes twice; I knew that much!

After I finished treating my blisters, I went over to the Moroccan tents. I figured they'd probably had some great strategies for keeping the sand out of their shoes. We got to talking and they invited me into their tent and graciously showed me their shoes. It was so simple. They had a bit of material covering the front part of their shoes to seal out the sand. That was it. It was so simple and yet the feet could still breath. There were racers who had parachute material all the way up to their knees to protect them from the sand. Why weren't we all doing it the way the Moroccans did?

That night, I waited for the results of stage three with baited breath. I finally decided that I'd rather not be in the top 50, but when they tabulated the results, there I was in 49th place.

I was both happy and disappointed. On the one hand, I thought if I hadn't made all those rookie mistakes, I could have done better. I also regretted having been so passive about it. I also considered that I might benefit from being grouped in with the majority of the racers, since I was still an inexperienced runner. After all, Marathon des Sables was turning out to be more of a learning experience than anything else. I realized I was second-guessing myself too much—an old habit—and I decided to quit it and just do my best from there on in.

The next morning, I woke up before everyone else in the Canadian tent. It was too good an opportunity to pass up.

"The Berbers are coming! The Berbers are coming!" I yelled.

The way everyone jumped up and started rolling up their sleeping pads and getting their gear together was hilarious.

I watched the bulk of the racers go out into the morning. It was strange to sit there at camp once all the tents had been removed. There was nothing to do but sit under the hot sun and wait.

We set off at noon. Within a couple kilometres, I met Simone Kaiser and her husband, and the three of us ran together for a stretch. They both knew that I was new to running and that it was my first time at Marathon des Sables. I kept commenting on how many people were passing us as we ran. I was beginning to feel concerned.

"Don't worry," Simone's husband said. "They'll slow down. Just maintain your pace; run at your own pace."

They both knew what they were talking about, so I took his advice and I didn't stress about other people's speed. I stuck to my own pace during that long day, and it turned out to be my best stage in the race.

I also remembered what Pat had told me about running in the sand during the long day. He had explained that after some trial and error, I would eventually find the sand that was more firmly packed and therefore provide the best footing. He told me to watch out for different wind patterns and shadows that that would help me to determine where the good sand was. It turned out he was right, but figuring it out was more art than science. Eventually, I got the hang of it.

Running behind the first 700 racers really gave me a lot more respect for the runners who usually hung back. I found it incredibly difficult to run in that chopped up sand. I realized how tough those runners really are.

Sometime in the middle of the day, I ran through a small village off the beaten track. I was surprised when all of the local kids started running behind us, waving and laughing. Since I was running through the village, I didn't have the time to really check it out, but just the kids alone gave me something to remember.

As the sky turned dark, I felt a second wind coming on. It was the first time I had experienced that. I'd been feeling really tired, almost sluggish, but then suddenly I started running faster than I had all day! It was awesome!

About 70K in, just 6K from the end of the fourth stage, my headlamp went out. To make matters worse, I ran right into a sand dune! It actually threw me off my feet. I crawled up the dune on my hands and knees, and when I made my way to the top, I looked off into the distance and saw the camp. I couldn't wait to get in. As I continued running, I noticed that every time I ran down a dune, the camp disappeared. I knew that meant I'd be running through a series of dunes for the last 5K. I was so exhausted that I'd literally scramble up the dune on my hands and knees and then run down to the bottom.

Once I'd made it over several dunes, I looked around for the race markers only to find that they had disappeared. I found out later that some of the local kids had removed them as a practical joke. By then, I was with a French runner by the name of Karim Mosta, and the two of us were completely disoriented. More specifically, we were lost. We lost site of camp and wandered around for a half hour before a support vehicle came and pointed us in the right direction. Thank God! I thought I might have had to sleep out there!

With the long day over, I went back to the Canadian tent. Some of the Canadians who started at 9 a.m. were there. After such a gruelling day, it was like a reunion to see my buddies! Mark and I laughed about how tough the day was. I collapsed onto my sleeping pad. As I lay there, I performed a mental checklist of my injuries. My feet felt like roast beef. My back looked like bubble wrap. My legs were chaffed from the tights, and I was off my food. With so much going wrong, I was surprised that I felt as happy as I did. There was nowhere else I'd rather be.

In retrospect, days like that forced me to push my body to a whole new level. I was tired out there, but I pushed the reset button and then found a *new* reset switch. My limits were all in my mind. I had tricked myself into believing I could only go so far. But we don't ever know what we're capable of until we push ourselves. It doesn't just apply to physical limits either. Once you go beyond what you ever thought you could do, there's no going back. It's with you forever. That was the most important lesson I learned at Marathon des Sables.

The rest of the race was pretty uneventful. After that ultramarathon stage, we had another marathon stage (a measly 42K that nearly kicked my ass) and then a ceremonial 20K finish on the last day. When it was over and I went through the finish line, I felt invigorated, as though I'd been injected with an education. I vowed to take everything I had learned at Marathon des Sables and apply to it to all my future races.

When the race was over, I asked Lisa Smith-Batchen whether she would consider coaching me. She had an online coaching program, and I knew that if I wanted to step up my game, Lisa would be the person to go to. She was incredibly busy, but she told me she'd think about it. I was thrilled!

I placed somewhere in the bottom 40s at Marathon des Sables, but I took 1$^{st}$ place out of the North American runners, which was incredible to me. I really wasn't expecting it, and when I found out, it felt great! There were so many incredible runners out there, so it was a real honour. I'd had an amazing time, met some really great people, and I knew, without a doubt, that I'd be coming back to the desert. I couldn't wait to see what I could really do!

# CHAPTER FOURTEEN

Dashing through the Alps
July 2004

W hen Marathon des Sables was over and I was back in Ottawa, I noticed that my recovery was a lot speedier than it had been after the Yukon Arctic Ultra. But I also noticed a change in my thinking. The first two races had been about merely finishing. Now I was thinking: What's next and how can I improve…how far can I push myself? In fact, it was almost *all* I could think about, even before I had convalesced enough to run again.

I felt good about Marathon des Sables. It was my own kind of glory. No, I hadn't won, but that wasn't the point. I had done my best under the circumstances, and I'd finished. That in itself was an accomplishment I was proud of, and the feeling that I was developing an identity was motivating. I was beginning to see that life wasn't a matter of wins and losses, as I had so long believed; it was more complex than that. My dreams and goals and ambitions were what defined me. And my dreams were getting big.

Shortly after I returned from Morocco, I received a call from Shirley Thompson, the woman I'd met on the way to our hotel in the Yukon (the one who'd thought I was a complete nut job). She wanted to tell me about the Jungle Marathon, a six-day stage race in the Amazon. She was the race organizer and was eager for me to participate.

"I'll give you your entry fee if you just get yourself out here," she told me. "Come on," she said, "I want you to do my race."

I was really flattered. Maybe a little terrified too. The

Amazon? The jungle? Uh-oh! As Shirley told me more about the race, I ignored my doubts and fears and thought about how amazing it would be to see that part of the world. I was really starting to get the hang of silencing that voice inside me that wanted to look at everything as though the glass were half empty. In the meantime, Shirley was more or less asking for a commitment on the spot.

I told her I'd do it, even though I didn't have a clue how I'd get myself out there. I'd have time to worry about that later though, since the race wasn't until mid-September. In the meantime, I had to concern myself with what was at hand. I'd actually made a huge commitment the year before to my buddy Nick Winfield. I'd promised to mountain bike with him in the Trans Alp.

It was strange to think about it. When I'd agreed to do the race in 2003, I hadn't discovered the ultramarathon. Back then, I had no way of knowing how ferociously I'd take up running. I wanted to focus on that, but I'd promised Nick I'd do the Trans Alp and there was no way I was going to back out. Nick called me about a week after I returned from Marathon des Sables.

"You ready to do this?" he asked

"Are you kidding me, man?" I said. "Bring it on!"

So back to the bike I went. At first it seemed a little foreign, as though it had been a very long time since I'd been on a bike, but I got comfortable again. The downside of biking was that I felt like I knew what my limits were. I'd been tested, so I knew for certain what my best was and how to get there. Running wasn't the same: I didn't know what I was capable of, so the possibilities were endless. Nevertheless, I knew I had to train, and train hard. I had help—Brian started biking with me too! He was actually going to be on the trip with Nick and I, although he wouldn't be racing.

By this time, I had gone back to work, and things were moving along smoothly. I had picked up some extra clients through Duane. He was still treating me, keeping me limbered up and my hip flexors loose, but occasionally he would refer some of his clients to me, and I'd work on strengthening their core. When I was working with Dr. Smith's clients, I would set up shop in one of the offices adjacent to his in the clinic.

One day, I was working with a client on the stability ball. As we were working on his technique, the door burst open and in walked a woman I'd never seen before. I looked up at her. She looked incredibly embarrassed.

"Oh my gosh, I'm so sorry!" she blurted.

I couldn't believe how cute she was! She had short blond hair and big blue eyes and the cutest nose I'd ever seen. The second I saw her I was instantly attracted.

"I'm not!" I said, because it was the first thing that came to mind, and also because it was true.

She turned around and left, closing the door behind her. My client laughed at my declaration, and then we tried to get back to work, but I couldn't concentrate. She kept popping up in my head.

After I finished with my client, I went over to the front desk. I knew Dr. Smith's secretary and hoped to pump her for some information about the woman I'd seen.

"Lynn," I said. "That girl, the blond who came into my office by accident—what do you know about her?"

Lynn gave me a bemused look: she'd never seen me express interest in anyone before, but then she admonished me.

"Ray, you know I'm not allowed to talk to you about Duane's clients."

Of course I knew that, but I didn't know what else to do! How else was I going to find out who she was?

"Listen," I said, "You've got to try to hook me up with this girl! You've got to find out if she has a boyfriend!"

Lynn said she'd try. That night, I went out for my usual run, but for the first time since I could remember, I had butterflies in my stomach.

I wanted to keep running, but I eventually had to stop entirely in order to focus all my training efforts on the Trans Alp. Nick and I started training together, and in order to even keep up with him, I had to put some serious training hours in. On the weekends, the two of us would go out for five or six hours at a time, and then do the same thing again on Sunday. It was a complete gearshift for me. No pun intended!

But I was excited too. I'd never been to that part of Europe and I was looking forward it. Also, I'd be racing against some of the best mountain bikers in the world. I knew that would be really cool.

The next time I went in to Duane's office, Lynn gave me some news. The girl I had seen that day was named Kathy and she didn't have a boyfriend. That was all she would tell me. Lynn had passed my number to Kathy and, I hoped, had recommended me. I also hoped Kathy would call.

I wasn't dating anyone. Sure, I'd gone out on a date or two, but I wasn't serious about anyone, and I'd come to accept that. It hadn't always been that way. The fact that I hadn't been in a serious relationship for years had been a source of pain for me, but I was getting much more comfortable with the idea that I might be alone forever. I think that change in attitude was brought on by my passion for running. It made me feel that my life was full and that I had exciting things on the horizon, with our without a girlfriend.

Or maybe I was fooling myself. Maybe I was using my new lifestyle as an excuse. I *did* have a crazy schedule and it *is* hard to meet anyone when you're always training or travelling, but it's also possible that I told myself that because I didn't want to feel like I was missing out. If I were honest with myself, I would know that in an ideal world, I'd meet someone who was passionate, caring, beautiful, and funny. I dreamed about it, but I was also willing to accept that it might never happen.

And then, a few weeks before I was to leave for Europe, I got a call from Kathy. She introduced herself and reminded me who she was—as if I could forget! We chatted away on the telephone for a couple of minutes and I asked her to meet me for coffee somewhere. We chose a Starbucks near her house in the Glebe.

With a knot in my stomach the size of a golf ball, I went to pick her up. I was so nervous! Would she like me? Would she think I was funny? Would she think I was cute?

She came to the door looking exactly as I'd remembered her, wearing jeans and a T-shirt. Something about her immediately put me at ease and I was able to put aside all my worries. We spent the next two or three hours in conversation—about what, I don't remember entirely. When I told her about my newly discovered passion for running, she was impressed. It turned out that Kathy had just taken up running herself. She told me about her family and her job and we shared a few laughs. I remember enjoying the sound of her laugh right away: it was infectious and boisterous and it made me want to hear it more. We talked until I had to leave to meet with a client.

It wasn't enough time, I wished I could stay and talk to her all day. I couldn't wait to see her again. Before I left for Trans Alp, I tried to see Kathy as many times as possible.

Each time I saw her, I felt more certain that I had met a very special person. On one of our early dates, we went hiking on a trail in Gatineau Park called Skyline. I couldn't believe my good fortune. Here I was, dating the woman of my dreams. She was cute, smart, and funny, and she actually *wanted* to go hiking with me!

In the meantime, I was truly excited about doing the Trans Alp. I knew that I was going to have a blast. The race would be sort of like the Marathon des Sables in that it was a stage race covering a total of 650K, but we would be racing in teams of two, and in some respects, the experience would be more relaxed. For one thing, we wouldn't be sleeping in the desert. Brian, along with Nick's wife, Andrea, would be trailing us in a rented camper, and when Nick and I had finished a stage, we'd be able to crash in there with them. And we didn't have to bring all our own food either, just what we'd need to eat while we were riding. Apart from that, we could eat at local establishments. Mike Edelson came through for me on a flight to Germany. I felt extremely fortunate to be sponsored by him. I also respected him a great deal: he was a self-made success, and I truly admired that. That was the kind of man I wanted to be.

The Trans Alp began in Mittenwald, Germany, where I had my first taste of a European deli. Just the smell of the deli, full of fresh breads and meats and cheeses, made my mouth water. As I loaded up on sandwiches, Brian went out to stock up on water for the race. He came back with cases of the cheapest bottled water he could find. Back at the camper, we discovered it was fizzy water! Poor Brian was forced to drink it himself for the rest of the trip.

Apart from that minor setback, we all had a great time. Deep down, I knew that the Trans Alp would be my last major bike race, so I wanted to give it my all. Still, just keeping up with Nick was a challenge. We'd ascend for 30K, which was tough enough, but the descents were way more challenging! We'd descend at 65 or 70 kph, sometimes more, and we were hardly the fastest descenders in the race either! I remember watching Nick take his hands off the handlebars to reach into his back pockets for food. Not me, I hung on for dear life!

Physically, I think the Trans Alp was one of the toughest things I've ever done. The climbs were monumental. Just to give you an idea, we did 24,000 metres of climbing over six stages! It was hard work, but I came away with nothing but good memories. At the end of each stage, Nick and I would hobble back to the camper and clean up, and then the four of us would go out in search of food. I ate extremely well during that trip. The six days we spent in the Alps were pretty simple: bike like hell, eat like pigs, sleep like babies.

One of the things that stands out in my memory is the start of the third day in Austria. We were about to do a major climb up a small mountain path. When the gun went off, over a thousand riders all gunned for the one narrow trail ahead. Within moments, you could hear a ton of brakes seizing up as riders slammed on their brakes, unable to get on the narrow trail in time. Once we were all in single file, I looked up to see that the trail zigzagged into the side of the mountain. All I could see was a single line of cyclists. I expected it to be tough, and put my bike into the lowest gear. That climb was *intense*: it took us hours to get up that mountain.

I should also admit that there were several occasions when I was scared out of my wits. I remember descending a mountain in Switzerland, going about 80 kph. I could see that there were tunnels carved straight into the mountain. The sun was bright and shining above us, and then, before I knew it, we were in sudden pitch darkness inside one of those tunnels. My eyes couldn't adjust to the darkness fast enough, so I couldn't see a damn thing! I was positive I was going to crash, but I couldn't put on the brakes, since we were still going downhill.

The race ended in Riva del Garda, Italy. As we made our way down the mountain, it started pouring rain. Within moments, we were all soaking wet. As I looked down at the finish line, I saw hundreds of people there waiting for us to come in. It seemed so European, all those people waiting to see the bikers! I couldn't get down there fast enough. When we crossed the finish line, I smiled so wide I think the ends of my mouth touched my ears! Everyone was cheering and stamping their feet. There were so many people that it felt like a party.

There, I thought, I'll never have to do that again! I was soaking wet, cold, and hungry, but happy as ever. I got off my bike and prepared myself for the biggest bowl of pasta in the world.

# CHAPTER FIFTEEN

Long May Your Big Jib Draw!
August 2004

I got back from the Trans Alp at the end of July. The Jungle Marathon wasn't until mid-September, so although I would be forced to once again switch disciplines, I had some time. I was too exhausted to start right away. I was eager to get back to work with my clients, but I didn't start my own training for another two weeks. I didn't want to push it. My body needed some well-deserved downtime.

That freed up some time to spend with Kathy. I'd thought about her a lot during the Trans Alp. I had wondered what she was doing, and I couldn't wait to get home and see her. I'd never felt that way before. While with anyone else, I'd always wondered if there was something else going on. I would wonder what I might be missing. Even spending the night at a girlfriend's house, I'd think about what the guys were up to. But that wasn't the case with Kathy. Whatever was happening was happening right there with her. Had I really met someone that I liked that much? It seemed too good to be true.

Kathy had been talking about taking a trip to Newfoundland to see her folks. When I got home, I suggested that we do that together. I wanted to see Newfoundland and meet the family I'd heard so much about. To hear Kathy talk, it was the greatest place on earth.

I was excited to meet her parents, John and Alice Adams, and see a new part of the country, but I was also pretty nervous. Meeting your girlfriend's parents is a big deal. I knew they'd be great; how could they not be when they'd raised someone like Kathy? But I wanted them to like *me*. I *really* wanted them to like me. It was nerve-wracking.

All my fears were assuaged the moment we got off the plane. Standing there in the airport were both of Kathy's parents. Her dad just looked nice. He had a very kind way about him and he hadn't spoken a word yet, and her mom looked very familiar. I could see Kathy in her mom's face right away. From the moment we met, they welcomed me into their lives as though I were already part of their family. Her mother gave me a giant hug and her father took my hand and shook it. I felt comfortable instantly. I didn't have to prove anything and that took all the pressure off. They were just like Kathy in that way.

The family lived in Harbour Grace, about an hour west of St. John's, but we passed through St. John's so I could have a look around. I was very impressed: I'd never seen anything like it. It was so colourful! The landscape was an array of bright colours: reds, oranges, pinks, blues, purples, and browns. Set against a backdrop of sea and sky, it was one of the most beautiful city skylines I'd ever seen.

I had vaguely expected Newfoundland to be cold and dreary, having read that the province receives the least amount of sunshine in Canada, but it was beautiful. I could see why the people chose to stay on what many think is an uninhabitable rock. I also loved the architecture. Many of the buildings and houses looked like they hadn't changed since the 1600s. There was something truly historic about it. I suppose this isn't all that surprising, since Newfoundland was the first English colony. Water Street in St. John's is the oldest street in North America!

When we got to Kathy's place, the house was bustling with people. Her oldest brother, Paul, a marine engineer, was there, as well as her sister Heather and brother-in-law Mick.

The only sibling missing was her brother Rob, who was travelling abroad. In this busy house, I got a sense of the kind of family that Kathy had come from. It was the sort of place where everyone is always welcome and people enjoy each other's company. There was no pretension.

Watching Kathy interact with her parents reminded me of just how great I thought she was. I couldn't put my finger on it exactly, although I knew I could articulate a hundred positive qualities about her. I loved how warm she was, how giving, that she was supportive and caring. I loved her attitude about life and her way of approaching things. We had a lot in common, but I also felt that our differences balanced us out. I've always been something of a dreamer and Kathy is more realistic. She grounded me, and maybe I made her dream a little.

Not long after we got back to the house, Kathy stepped out to walk across the property to visit with her aunt and uncle. As people buzzed around the house, chatting and laughing, preparing food or eating, Paul gave me a mischievous look. Before I knew it, he had whisked me out of the house, and we travelled across the harbour to a nearby tavern. We got to know each other over a couple of beers while a live band played sea shanties. It was awesome!

Kathy and I stayed in Newfoundland for a week. In that time, I had more fish than you could shake a stick at. I also had a sampling of some of the traditional dishes: moose sausage, fish and brewis, salt cod. I even had a jigg's dinner: a dish with salt beef, potatoes, and peas puddin'.

On our last day there, we went out whale watching in Bay Bulls. We signed up with a tour and went out on an old decommissioned fishing boat painted green on the bottom and white on the top. Of course, there weren't any icebergs in August, but I wished I could have seen some. Kathy's parents had shown me a few pictures, and in some ways, they reminded me of the dunes in Morocco. They were so huge and regal. One of the things I love about dunes or icebergs is how enormous yet pure they are. They are so much themselves and they stand so proud out there on their own.

I also hoped to see some humpback whales, but Kathy's mom told me they were very rare in August, so I looked out for the next best thing: the minke whale, a smaller variety. Unfortunately, I didn't see any of those either. I think that might have been my fault though—I kept looking at Kathy. It's just that she seemed so in her element, with the wind in her hair and the smell of the sea in the air. As we cruised along the water, I couldn't keep my eyes off of her.

Still, I couldn't help noticing the puffins, which were literally everywhere. There were thousands of them, hanging out on the cliffs, flying low over the water, diving into the sea and grabbing fish in their orange beaks. They were so cute, too, with their little black tuxedos and their bright orange legs.

That trip on the boat was also the first time I heard about, and took part in, a screech-in ceremony. Since then, I've been screeched-in twice. A screech-in is a traditional ceremony that everyone on the island knows about: it's how visitors become honorary Newfoundlanders. The ceremony usually involves a bottle of screech (a high-octane rum) and kissing a codfish.

In my case, it was the captain of the boat who offered to host the ceremony. Instead of a codfish, however, they had a stuffed toy puffin. It was a festive atmosphere: music blasted from the speakers, I kissed the puffin on the arse, and the captain declared, "Long may your big jib draw!"

Everyone cheered. Frankly, I had no idea what it meant, but it seemed like a very good thing.

# Chapter Sixteen

The Race of Attrition
September 2004

I prepared myself as best I could for the Jungle Marathon. As for gear, I was good to go, and in terms of running, I was more or less ready. I was still an inexperienced runner, but I had learned a lot from Marathon des Sables. I knew I could run the distance—it was over 200K—but everything else was a crapshoot. I had no clue how to live in the jungle, and I wasn't prepared to face whatever monsters would be out there.

I was instructed to get many different shots to protect myself against disease. I had shots for hepatitis A and B, yellow fever, and rabies (in case I was bit by a monkey!) in addition to anti-malarials—everything you can and should get from a travel doctor in Canada.

Then it was a question of getting there. The flight, after all my connections, took me over thirty hours. I flew from Ottawa to Toronto, Toronto to Miami, Miami to São Paolo, and from there I flew to Belém. Finally, on a small carrier aircraft, I flew to Santarém, a market city midway between Belém, the chief port of the Amazon Basin, and Manaus on the lower central Amazon.

We landed on a tiny airstrip in the middle of the night. I was the first racer there. One of Shirley's assistants, Monica, picked me up at the airport. As we drove down the dirt road towards the hotel, I was shocked to see that the roads were teeming with people on foot. It was pitch dark. Shirley's assistant explained that because of the daytime heat, it was much easier and more comfortable to get around at night.

Even at night, the temperatures were extremely high: it was nearly 40°C and the air was wet with humidity. I couldn't imagine how much worse it was going to get in the light of day. The roads were total disasters, crawling with snakes and hard to navigate—we were, after all, at the edge of the jungle.

I was extremely happy to get to the hotel. With its proximity to the jungle, it was a hub of activity: scientists, tourists, and anyone else who had reason to go into the jungle stayed there. The rooms themselves were very rudimentary, consisting of a bed, a TV, and a window, but they had the essentials, and I didn't need anything else. Other than the rooms, everything was open concept. Meals were taken under a thatched roof shelter with poles keeping the ceiling up. The dining area was a large space, big enough to accommodate over a hundred people. I'd never been to a place where almost all the structures were completely open like that; there were no walls at all!

The next day, as some of the other racers starting filing in, the atmosphere got more intense. I had my first real taste of Brazilian cuisine that day, as I snacked on grilled chicken and even tried some barbequed alligator. The alligator wasn't as exotic as I had expected—it tasted like chicken—but I loved the grilled pineapple dish I tried for dessert.

Through Shirley, I found out that Robert Pollhammer, the course designer for the Yukon Arctic Ultra, had also been hired to chart out the course for the jungle. Robert's races are notoriously difficult, so I was a little frightened. I knew the Jungle Marathon was going to be a serious adventure.

I was glad to find that I knew several of the racers there, including Jay Batchen, Lisa's husband. I'd asked Lisa if she would be willing to coach me back at the Marathon des Sables. When I saw Jay, he delivered good news: Lisa had thought it over and decided to take me on. I was overjoyed!

I'd never really had a coach before. That Lisa wanted to coach me meant that she believed in me. That meant the world to me.

Jay also invited me to join his team for the Jungle Marathon. I had originally planned to run the race solo, but Jay explained that joining a team wouldn't effect my individual time. Teams were grouped in fours, and the fastest cumulative time of all four runners would win in the team category. I totally wanted to be on a team with Jay. It would include two other runners that I had heard a lot about: Kevin Lin and Charlie Engle, both notoriously strong runners.

Charlie hadn't made it to the hotel yet, but Kevin was already there. He was like a rock star in Taiwan, known for his incredible strength and endurance. I saw him later that day sitting by the pool. I went over to introduce myself, and I asked him about the tattoo he had on his back. It was written in Arabic script, so I recognized it, but I didn't know what it meant. Kevin explained that it read: "an eye for an eye." We sat by the pool and chatted. He was totally cool. He might be a rock star in Taiwan, but he sure doesn't act like one.

The next day we set out for camp. Charlie still hadn't made it to Santarém, and people were starting to wonder whether he'd make it at all. The hotel was located about 50K from the Tapajós River, a huge body of water that pours into the Amazon. When we got to the edge of the river, two old-school diesel-burning steamboats greeted us. We were told that the starting line was located nearly ten hours away. We all piled into the boats—there were about a hundred of us, including the medical crew, race organizers, and volunteers.

After about an hour of chugging along, my T-shirt was completely soaked from the humidity and I started to feel like my head was going to explode. It was the diesel fumes. I got down on the floor of the boat and closed my eyes. I was so far from home, going deeper and deeper into the jungle. I wasn't sure if I had done the right thing.

After a gruelling ten-hour boat ride, we got into camp. Well, near camp. The boat couldn't dock because the waters were too shallow, so we all jumped into the river. With my pack above my head, I gingerly waded through the waters, certain that at any moment something fierce and hungry would reveal itself—and its teeth—to me. As I made my way towards land, I thought about the release forms I had signed. *Why* did I sign them again? What exactly did I get myself into? What was I going to be coming up against in the jungle? What if I was attacked by a poisonous insect, or snake, or frog, or God knows what else?

Out of the water, we walked past the beach and up a steep sandy slope. When I saw the camp, my jaw nearly dropped. What Shirley had done was truly amazing. She had used local materials to build a huge meeting centre. The idea was that we would use this place as a base camp during the race before handing it over to the locals so they could use it as a community centre, to bring in tour groups, or to host town meetings. It struck me as a truly generous thing to do, considering there was no way the race had brought in enough money to pay for what Shirley had built.

There were two main pavilions, both large enough to host nearly a hundred people, each with a thatched roof made of palm leaves and held upright by poles dug deep into the ground. It was open and airy with rows and rows of picnic tables. At the end of the first building, a rudimentary kitchen and an area for food preparation had been erected. Beside that there was another large structure, this one strung up with hammocks for the racers. The hammocks were sealed with mosquito netting, which made them look like cocoons. Then there were the smaller buildings, one of which we used for gear check-in the following day. But the truly amazing thing is that Shirley had built outhouses—with rudimentary plumbing and all—and had made sure to keep it all easy to maintain and repair.

It was getting late by the time we got to camp. Everyone was wearing their headlamps, mingling around, meeting the other racers, organizing their packs, and sorting gear. We were a very international bunch, and I met a lot of runners from all over the world, including Freddie Olmquist from Sweden, an incredibly fast trail runner, and Banjo, a hilarious super-tough ex-cop from Ireland. There were also a lot of Brazilian runners. Shirley had allowed the Brazilians to compete without an entry fee because she felt strongly about the locals being able to compete in their own country. But many of them didn't have adequate gear or shoes, and some of them had no gear whatsoever. In fact, many of them would be running in flip-flops!

Jay introduced me to a friend of his, a guy named Dari from Israel. Dari was talking about how he had the greatest thing to keep the mosquitoes away. A few minutes later, as Jay and I were on our way to get some food, we ran into Dari. There he was, his arm leaned up against a railing on the side of a hut, wearing a suit made out of the kind of mosquito netting that usually goes around the bottom of a hat, except that this thing covered his entire body. Underneath it, he was naked except for a small pair of black briefs. It was one of the most ludicrous things I'd ever seen in my life. Jay and I started to laugh so hard neither of us could catch our breath. Meanwhile, Dari just stood there, with a completely serious look on his face. That guy was too much!

The next day, we did gear check-in, which was a good thing because all of us needed a day to recuperate from the travel and long boat ride. After that, we were treated to a jungle marathon training camp, a kind of "what to expect in the jungle" seminar. We were briefly acquainted with a bunch of different deadly snakes, poisonous insects, and told to be on the look out for wild boars, jaguars, and even the poison arrow frog!

Before the seminar was over, they told us that the next day's race would only be 14K. I breathed a heavy sigh of relief. Only 14K? I figured I'd be done in less than two hours. I was dead wrong.

Early the next morning, we all gathered under the start banner, ready to begin the race. Charlie still wasn't there, so I figured we wouldn't be participating in the event after all. In front of us, the jungle looked ominous. It was so dense and dark. The sand under my feet was gritty, a strange texture I wasn't familiar with. It was the opposite of the fine, soft sand in the Sahara. The air was extremely hot and humid, and it made me sweat just standing there. It had a pungent scent to it and smelled thick with soil and life.

Just as we were about to start the race, we heard the sound of a helicopter overhead. Shirley had commissioned them, in case of emergency, and now one was being used to fly Charlie in. The helicopter dropped Charlie off and he ran over to the start line and greeted our team. So that's where I met Charlie, on the start line. I was so glad he had made it! I knew that Charlie was a great adventure racer, and that the Jungle Marathon was exactly his kind of race. I was beginning to get the feeling that this race was as much about fitness as it was about technique, and as much about gear as it was about jungle experience. Charlie had it all, so I told him I was going to try to stick by him as long as I could.

The gun went off. Within minutes, Kevin, Charlie, Freddie, a few Brazilian runners, and I were out in front, sprinting down the beach. We suddenly came head to head with a wide body of water that we had to cross. I'm not much of a swimmer, but I thought: what the hell? I cleared my mind, jumped in, and started swimming across to the other side.

As soon as the water crossing was over I saw a wall of jungle. Every type of vegetation you could possibly imagine was there: trees with leaves the size of bed sheets, and vines hanging everywhere and criss-crossing on the trail, just waiting to catch your foot. There was grass so sharp that if you brushed up against it, it would cut right through your shorts and skin. All this plant life was just waiting to get you, and yet, at the same time, it was intensely beautiful. As soon as I left the beach and entered the jungle, I saw that the rustling in the leaves had disturbed a bright blue butterfly and it flew up and over me.

I was thoroughly soaked and knew there was no way my shoes were ever going to dry in the humidity. I tried to run but found the terrain extremely difficult. There was so much happening! I tried to be as light on my feet as I could, but I wasn't used to it. I felt at a great disadvantage attempting to negotiate the trail as I stumbled all over the place. When I looked up, I realized that I had gone totally off course. That was when I was glad that I had paid attention during the seminar. I stopped, and started walking back to the last place I recognized. I eventually saw tape, and knew I was back on the trail. I had lost the group though, and was now on my own.

I was surprised to find that the jungle was hilly. Once back on the course, I found myself on a major mud slope. It was so steep that I literally had to get onto my hands and knees and claw my way up.

It didn't take me long to realize that Newton's law of gravity was in full effect here. Every time you went up a hill, you would inevitably go down into a swamp, which is just what happened when I finally made my way up to the top of the first steep slope. No sooner had I clawed my way up did I start falling down the other side, on my ass, right into a swamp!

It was full of mud. The roots from the enormous trees surrounding it formed what looked like a cage over the water. There was a mist above it and a canopy of crazy trees and vines hanging down, forming U-shapes over the water, almost like hydro lines that had come down in an ice storm. As I waded through the thick water, I wondered what kinds of horrible monsters I was about to run into and when the alligators were going to show up.

While I tried to make my way across the swamp, a Brazilian runner joined me. Neither of us could speak one another's language, but we communicated wordlessly and worked our way out of the swamp together. I was glad to have him there.

By the end of the first day, three people had already dropped out, and I knew it was going to one tough race. Even Charlie admitted that it was the hardest first leg of a race he'd ever done. As for me, after 14K in the jungle, I already knew it wasn't my thing. As beautiful as it was, I would have given anything to be back in the desert.

That's what the first day was all about for me: getting used to the idea that you were always going to be muddy, wet, surrounded by vegetation, and, perhaps most important, that you were always going to be a little freaked out.

When we got into camp that night, we all concerned ourselves with stringing up our hammocks and preparing our dinners. The Jungle Marathon was like Marathon des Sables in terms of food, except that they provided us with hot water for our dehydrated meals. We were camped near a group of trees. The ground was covered in fallen branches, weed, and sand, and no one dared walk on the ground with bare feet for fear of scorpions. People had already seen a few. I strung up my hammock and removed my shoes. My feet were caked with mud and they looked pretty beat up. There was no way anything was going to dry overnight, and I started wondering what kinds of funky rashes we'd all end up with after a week of wet clothes and shoes.

I slept poorly in the hammock all sealed up like that. I actually awoke several times to find that I had turned over on my side in my sleep and that the whole hammock had flipped over. It was a strange thing, waking up upside down! And it severely sucked, I might add.

The second day was just under 24K and the terrain was equally as difficult as on the first day. I couldn't find a rhythm. At one point, my right foot started to hurt in the area near my big toe. I didn't want to stop and take my shoes off in the middle of the trail, so I tried to ignore it. I figured I probably had a blister—something you can't do anything about anyway.

I knew there was a checkpoint coming up, so I pressed on. That's when I heard a strange rustling sound behind me. I wasn't sure what it was. I went through a list of animals in my mind. Could it be a jaguar? The sound got louder and louder, and then I heard grunting. I turned around and saw a brown streak of colour racing behind me. It was a wild boar running down the trail! I took off running as fast as my legs would take me, winding down the narrow path. I heard crashing and grunting behind me and I sped up. My heart was pounding and I couldn't feel my legs.

When I saw a checkpoint ahead, I screamed, "Wild boar! Behind me!"

The volunteers in the camp didn't seem to hear me. I kept running like mad towards the checkpoint. I saw two Brazilian guys doubled over in laughter. I turned around and saw that there was nothing behind me. The boar had come onto the trail for just a few moments and then had disappeared back into the jungle. Once my panic subsided, I realized that the imaginary boar had actually forced me to go way faster than I had thought I could go: it was a blessing in disguise.

That night, I took off my shoes and socks to inspect my injured foot. My feet were so wrinkled they looked like they'd been in a bathtub for a week. Plus I had some major blisters. There was a faint purple colour deep in the knuckle on my big toe. I went to the first-aid station and asked the doctor to take a look at it.

He told me I had an abscess in my toe and that he'd have to freeze it and dig in there to get it out.

"But you know the risks, right? The minute we cut into you, you're opening your body up to all kinds of infections," the doc said.

What could I do? I could barely run on it.

"We gotta do it," I told him.

He gave me antibiotics, put my foot to sleep, and then cut into the toe. What a relief. Unfortunately, he had had to dig in deep to get at the thing, and my foot was pretty damaged. He wrapped my toe up and altered the inside of my shoe to take the pressure off it, but it was still in bad shape.

By the next morning, the camp looked like a battle zone. The racers were dirty, wet, blistered, and incredibly tired. Several more people dropped out of the race, and by the end of that day, eighteen racers had dropped out.

The day's course was 31K and it was full of mud and hills and water crossings. When I got my foot wet, I could feel water and sand rushing in and out of my blisters. The skin under the ball of my foot was starting to rub off too.

Making my way through another swamp - Jungle Marathon

And there was nothing to be done. You couldn't tape up your feet because of the moisture.

My battle against the pain was intense. I kept reminding myself that I was on a team, which helped. I wanted to do well for myself, but I also didn't want to let my team down. By the fourth day, however, which was 21K, it got harder to think that way. Every step hurt. Every water crossing made it worse. I wanted to quit.

I was on a rough trail, and the pain in my feet wasn't getting any better. In fact, it was excruciating. I thought about stopping. I knew that my battered feet were a good enough excuse to bail. No one would blame me or say I had copped out. I imagined myself giving up on the race, putting my feet up, just letting them heal. I stopped running and began to walk. I had a choice. I didn't *have* to run. I could stop—I wanted to stop—but I knew that I hadn't truly pushed myself to the point where I couldn't go any longer.

It occurred to me that after all those years of being afraid to fail, I didn't even know what real failure was. I wouldn't be a failure if I couldn't complete the race! I could only fail if I gave up on myself, if I sold myself short. I could still run, and I could walk if I had to. I could learn to adapt and deal with the pain. And that's what it came down to: I could give up on myself or I could keep on going.

I wasn't going to give up on myself. I would drop from exhaustion before that ever happened. I picked up my pace and ran the rest of the course.

The fifth day was by far the longest, toughest, and most memorable leg of the race. It was 85K, we had thirty-six hours to complete it, and it began at 4 a.m.

It started with a long swim across a river. It was still dark out. There was a mist on the water. Charlie and Kevin were faster swimmers than me, and by the time I made it to the other side, they were well ahead of me. I found some other people to run with, however: an Italian, a Brit, and a Spanish guy. The four of us managed to get lost as soon as we got out of the water. When we found the right trail, we saw that it lead up a very steep climb.

As we made our way up the trail, the sun began to break. Suddenly, I heard Chris, the British racer, screaming.

"*Run!*" he yelled, so we all started running, no questions asked. I quickly discovered that we were being chased down by a swarm of wasps. They got us all, everywhere. Chris was stung on the side of the head. I got it in the legs and arms. The most aggressive of them were going straight for our eyes! We ran like hell, and I narrowly escaped a severe beating from those things.

We carried on. For hours, we wound through trails, went

in and out of swamps, and avoided vines and bamboo shoots as sharp as knives. Finally, we came to a checkpoint, where the staff told us we had made it in time to go through. Many other racers would not be allowed to continue because this patch of jungle was the area most highly populated with jaguars. Racers who came after dark would have to stop for the night. The clock would stop and they would be allowed to start again the next day. It smelled incredibly musky out there, like urine, which we were told was the scent of the jaguars.

The four of us power-walked because the terrain was too dense to run through. We knew those damn cats were out there, we could smell them, but we couldn't see them. It was spooky. Finally, the jungle opened and dumped out onto a trail that continued to get wider until it turned into a road made of deep sand. I had probably been running for fifteen hours by then. I was glad to be out of the jungle, but I was dehydrated and hungry. I couldn't keep up with the Italian and Spanish guy, and they took off, leaving Chris and I to fend for ourselves.

I realized that the Italian racer had accidentally made off with my headlamp, which I had put in the back of his pack during a water crossing. I knew it had been unintentional, but as it started to get dark, I worried—I needed my headlamp. We eventually teamed up with a Brazilian runner named Andrea, who spoke Portuguese. This became a huge benefit to us because when we made our way into a village and got lost, she was able to speak to the local villagers and find out how to get back on course. At about 20K from the finish, we came into a checkpoint where I saw the Italian runner. He wasn't feeling too hot and was resting. I got my headlamp back from him, and we pressed on.

I was incredibly glad to have my headlamp back, except

for when it illuminated the biggest furriest tarantula I had ever seen. I caught sight of it just as I was about to step on it. It was right under my foot, staring up at me. It was the size of my palm, with little flecks of orange colours in its fur. My heart stopped. Oh shit! There wasn't enough time to think: just as my foot was about to stomp its life out, it scurried out of the way. The tarantula was okay, but I was shaken. I'd seen snakes and I'd seen insects, and those things hadn't really affected me, but the tarantula actually scared me. I couldn't stop thinking about it. I was still thinking about it later when we crossed the next swamp and the light of my lamp shone into the water, exposing the eyes of a bunch of caymans. I swam like hell.

I heaved myself out of the water and rolled down the beach toward the finish line. Right before the end of the course, I passed through a small section of dense woods. I remembered the advice given to me by a friend of mine who had completed an eco-challenge in Borneo. He had told me to *never* shine my headlamp into the woods at night. As I ran through the jungle, I kept repeating this to myself over and over again…do not look in the woods, do not look in the woods….

But of course I did! What I saw was a million little eyes looking back at me, reflecting off the light of my headlamp. Every size and shape of eye stared back at me: big ones, little ones, round ones, diamond ones. In my tired state, I believed all of those eyes belonged to creatures that wanted to eat me. So *that's* why he didn't want me looking into the woods, I thought. Later, I was told that the diamond-shaped eyes were tarantulas. I'd seen a lot of those. Just thinking about it made me shiver with fear.

I finished in 7th place that night. There was only a small group of us that made it to camp by then, every one else had to be pulled off the course. I was exhausted! I ate as much of

Wading through a water crossing - Jungle Marathon

my food as I could. I was probably only eating a total of 3,500 calories a day, so I was always running at a deficit. I promised myself that from there on in, I would bring more food with me, damn the weight.

The next day, we had the day off as we waited for the rest of the runners to come in. Although I don't usually think it's good to stop for too long during a stage race, I was badly in need of some rest. That said, spending the day off my feet was probably not a great idea, since the lack of circulation caused them to swell even more. I had no idea how I was going to get through the last day. It seemed impossible.

Nevertheless, when we started out on the final leg of the race, I put it all behind me. It was as though I suddenly developed tunnel vision. There was no way I was going to let my feet stop me. I wanted to get to that finish line way too much. When the gun went off, I started sprinting, and decided I would not stop running, no matter what, until I made it to the finish line.

I had 25K to go. I ran along the beach the whole day, even getting attacked by wasps again. I kept going. The beach eventually opened up and I saw a cruise boat in the water. I saw people laying out on the beach, tanning. It was surreal. From the jungle to civilization, all within hours. I wanted to lie down in the sun too, but I kept going.

I ignored the pain in my feet until I noticed that the pain just disappeared! It was the strangest thing: I truly could not feel *anything*. I was running on pure adrenaline. I had mentally driven myself to the point where I could no longer tolerate the pain and it just went away. After some time, I saw a village ahead of me, and then a series of steps. I ran up to the top of the steps and then, there at the top, I saw a banner. It was over. I had made it! I couldn't believe it. The pain in my feet returned almost as soon as the race was done. They started to throb, but I didn't care—I had run through the jungle and lived to tell the tale.

The most relaxing part of the experience came next, when we were told to meet at the beach for a ceremony and celebration. From the beach, we were shuttled out in boats to an island that Shirley had rented for the night. There was a ton of food and drink, and those of us who could, spent the night dancing.

Our team won for fastest group, and Charlie and Kevin took 1st and 2nd place respectively. I'd made eighth. It was awesome! I thanked Shirley for the opportunity to complete the toughest race I'd ever done. It had been torture, and it had been painful, but I'd come for an adventure, and I'd definitely had one. I was happy it was over, but I was even happier that I hadn't given up.

My feet were so swollen that I spent several days in the

hotel in Santarém with bags of ice packed around my feet, using a cane to walk. They were so swollen, I couldn't fit them into my shoes, and so I was concerned about getting on a series of long flights.

My flight home was an adventure all on its own. In Belém, we were told that the next connection had been cancelled and that we'd be stuck in São Paolo for at least two days. I couldn't stand the thought of being away any longer! I yearned to back at home, to get out of the humidity and back to Canada. I managed to make friends with an airline employee who sympathized with my predicament. She looked around and found me another flight, and before long, I was on my way back to Ottawa.

When I got home, I noticed that there was a smell coming from my feet. A funky infected kind of smell. That's weird, I thought. I can smell my feet all the way over here where my head is. It didn't seem right. I knew there were pockets of infection under my feet. I had blisters full of puss under the skin. It was totally gross.

A couple of weeks later, when Kathy was on a business trip in Kingston, I noticed that the back of my leg was hurting. When I checked it out, I saw what looked like a boil, or a big flat hive the size of my fist on my hamstring. It was black in the centre. After a few hours, it started to swell. Eventually, the thing got to be about the size of a football. I woke up with a fever the next day. I felt delusional. I took myself over to the ER immediately. When they told me it would be a six-hour wait, I leaned over the desk and quietly told the nurse that I'd just come back from a week in the Amazon jungle.

That got things moving a lot faster.

"We'll get someone out to see you immediately," she told me.

Running through the dense Amazon - Jungle Marathon

The doctors had me lay out on my stomach while they poked around at the back of my leg, but no one knew exactly what it was. They assumed it was some kind of infection, but they weren't sure what. Finally, I was given some antibiotics and sent home.

Unfortunately, the antibiotics didn't work. About a week later, something strange started growing on my lower back. It was the same thing: it started off looking like a hive, then started to swell. This time, though, the whole thing turned black. When one of my clients—a doctor—saw it, he warned me to get back to the hospital. I took his advice, but I was already light headed and feverish. Still, no one at the hospital knew what to make of it. I kept taking the antibiotics.

Kathy and Brian both helped me out with this strange thing growing on my back, since I couldn't reach it. They'd clean it out and tend to it. One day, Brian was working on it, scrubbing at it to keep it clean, when he started to inspect it more carefully.

"It looks like something's trying to get out of there," he said.

As he poked away it, a massive lump of puss about the size of my thumb came out. It was so disgusting! The remaining hole was as deep as my knuckle. We sent it away to a lab and found out later it was a parasitic infection! Once it was out of my body, I felt much better. I shoved gauze deep into the hole to keep it plugged up, and then got to the task of training for the Trans 333.

# CHAPTER SEVENTEEN

The Race of Intention
November 2004

I heard about the Trans 333 through Shirley at the Jungle Marathon. It sounded wild. It had no fixed location, you used GPS devices to navigate your way through the terrain, and it was 333K non-stop! The race was supposed to provide food and water, but Shirley warned me from the very beginning to prepare for it as though it were completely self-sufficient, as though they weren't going to be giving you anything at all.

Trans 333 was nowhere near as famous as some of the bigger races like Marathon des Sables or Badwater, but it had a reputation amongst runners as being one hell of a race. You never knew what would happen. Because of its relative anonymity, it didn't have the same kind of money and sponsorships as the bigger races, so it was more like an indie race, if you will. Alain Gestin had a reputation as a tough but hilarious race director, if not maybe a bit laissez-faire.

There was something about the Trans 333 that sounded romantic to me. Shirley encouraged me to try it out and told me that this year's race would be somewhere in Niger. No one knew exactly where, but it would be in the Ténéré region of the Sahara Desert. I wanted to get back there badly. Just that amount of information was enough to get me to send in my race application. I still wore the necklace I got in Morocco, the cross of Agadez. I sent my forms in and then didn't hear back from anybody for a while.

Eventually, I received word to make my way to Orly, one of the two major airports in Paris. I was told which terminal to go to after that, but I didn't know which flight I'd be on. They said they'd give you your tickets from there. It was like *Mission: Impossible.*

When I got to Orly, I found the right terminal, but I had no clue what was going on. I called Kathy from a payphone in the airport and told her I didn't know when I'd be able to call her again. It really was shaping up to look like an adventure!

I spied some people at the terminal who looked vaguely familiar. They were all wearing running gear, so I approached them. Most of them were French runners and didn't speak English. Finally, I met Wayne Simpson, who took on the nickname "The Dragon of Leeds," and another runner named Jack Denness. Jack was legendary. He'd completed the Badwater Ultramarathon in Death Valley over ten times. Badwater was billed as one of the toughest footraces in the world.

We flew from Paris to Agadez. We were a small group of racers; there were only about forty of us. When we landed and I looked out the window, I knew I had come to an incredibly remote part of the world. The airstrip was hardly big enough to contain our plane. The airport itself was like a concrete shell. The heat was intense too, and the smell—it reminded me of Morocco. But whereas Morocco had hints of Europe in the architecture, Niger did not. This was the remote Sahara. As we drove through Agadez, I was amazed. It's one of the biggest cities in Niger, but there were no traffic lights and few paved roads. The buildings were all made of clay. The air was thick with the smell of exhaust fumes and the streets were filled with old Land Cruisers and people on small scooters. I fingered my necklace as we made our way through the dusty streets. By our standards—by any standards—this was an amazingly poor city.

A camel train in the Sahara

Driving around Agadez, I couldn't help but think how amazing it was that a culture such as the Touaregs had somehow remained intact after all these thousands of years. Something about these people immediately affected me and I felt the need to connect with them. Also, driving through the city, I couldn't help but think of how diseases such as malaria were still so rampant. It just didn't seem fair.

The racers, organizers, and our Touareg guides all climbed into Land Cruisers and drove out into the desert. The Touareg are desert folk. They have a long nomadic history in North and West Africa. The Touareg guides were dressed in extremely colourful robes, and they all wore very ornate silver jewellery. I thought they looked extraordinary. They were all tall and dark, with very fine noble faces. They seemed to have a truly generous friendly nature and were so gentle.

We drove 333K out into the desert. The idea was that we would run back into the city. The trip took us two days, and we stopped halfway through to sleep. The next day we made it to our destination: the L'Arbre du Ténéré, or, in English, the Tree of Ténéré.

Actually, it wasn't really a tree. It was a monument to the last standing tree in that region of the Sahara. Legend has it that the lone tree had survived for decades out there in the parched desert until it was badly damaged by an incompetent driver and had to be moved. But the tree's existence in that dry place for so long was almost like a miracle. No one knew how it had survived out there. I imagined the tree's struggle in the face of true adversity.

There was absolutely nothing else around the monument but a lone well. The desert was amazingly vast. All I could see for miles around me was sand, sand, and more sand. I couldn't imagine running all the way back to Agadez. We would begin the following morning at 4:30 a.m.

I had brought fifteen drop-bags full of food, gels, bars, and anything else I'd thought I might need at each of the checkpoints. The idea was that you would strap on a pre-programmed GPS system to your wrist and use that as your guide. Checkpoints were stationed approximately every 23K.

It was still dark when we started to race. The wind blew cool air onto our faces that morning, but it didn't last long. When the sun came up, it got incredibly hot. I started out with the lead pack of runners. The first few checkpoints went by almost unnoticed, but somewhere around the 66K mark, a sandstorm blew in. I was wearing an MP3 player and listening to Fatboy Slim when I first noticed the wind kicking up. At first the sand was up at my ankles and then at my knees. It was pretty amazing! I cranked my tunes and ran against it, but I remember breathing a silent prayer that my GPS didn't screw up.

I did my best to stay with the more experienced runners. Jack and Wayne were an incredible source of information

Alone in a crazy sandstorm - Trans 333

for me. They had a lot of experience and I learned as much as I could from them before the race started. I would not see them again until the race was over.

The desert in Niger was different than Morocco: in many ways, it was more intense. The wind was constant and strong, and the sand it kicked up actually took the lamination off my sunglasses. I also found the sand more difficult to run under.

After the sandstorm, I found myself alone, and it stayed like that for the majority of the race. I had so much time to reflect on the beauty of the desert. I saw sand dunes and beautiful night skies. The sheer size of the desert and its emptiness was a thing of wonder to me. When I got too tired to go on, I pulled my bivy sack out of my pack and crawled inside to sleep for ten or fifteen minutes. I worried about scorpions, but I was too exhausted to let it stop me. My strategy was to get the first 160K done in about twenty-four hours, so I definitely didn't want to sleep for too long. At

The Touareg of Niger

one point, I saw a truck full of armed men driving through, but I didn't stop to chat.

I also saw a train of camels—maybe fifty of them—walking with a group of nomads. Everyone smiled and waved at me as I ran by them. It was amazing to witness this group of people out there in the desert, people who were literally living off the land. Their resilience amazed me. I thought *I* was tough, running this race, but that's when I

Accepting my award: a Touareg cross - Trans 333

realized that these people were the truly strong ones.

As I plodded by this group of nomads, a young girl ran up behind me. She was little, maybe just seven or eight years old. I didn't know what she wanted, but I had two water bottles in the back of my pack, and when she started grabbing at one, I took it out and gave it to her. It didn't have much water left, just a few drops, so I thought that perhaps she wanted to play with the bottle. When I ran into the next checkpoint, I told one of the Touareg guides about it. He told me that she probably hadn't had any clean water all day. It was the first time I had truly thought about what that could be like. I had never thought in those terms before. There really wasn't enough water around, and the little that was available wasn't clean. The image of this small girl, with her sweet face and big eyes, followed me all the way back to Agadez. In fact, I never forgot her. I don't think I ever will.

In the last third of the race, around 230K, I spotted an Italian runner named Max coming towards me in a Land Cruiser. He had injured his knee pretty badly and was forced to drop out the race. He'd come back just to let me know that I was now in 2nd place!

I was totally excited but also exhausted and sore. With the help of my MP3 player and the beauty of the desert, I kept on going, only stopping very occasionally for short naps. The time passed and I went forward, luckily never getting lost or going off course. When I got into a checkpoint around the 300K mark, Alain Gestin was there.

"You're doing really good," he said, pointing out that I was still in 2nd place, "but you should not wait. There is someone behind you." Last year's winner, a French runner named Theo, was in 3rd place. I'd been running solo for so many hours, I actually relished the company.

"You know, I've run almost this whole race alone. I wouldn't mind running with someone, especially someone who's won before," I told Alain.

Alain shrugged.

"Okay," he said. "It's your choice. Whatever happens, happens."

I waited a few minutes for Theo to show up.

"Do you want to run together or race this last 33K? If we run together, we can share second place," I offered.

Theo wanted to run together. I waited for him to have a bite to eat, and then we took off. We were both tired, so we did a lot of walking and talking. It was good to be in the company of another person again.

We had watched night turn to day twice. Now it started

to get dark again. I could almost see the outskirts of Agadez in the distance, but the air was dusty and it was hard to make out anything clearly. I stopped to look at the cityscape. That's when I noticed that my headlamp had stopped working. I looked down at my GPS and saw that it was also dying. I tried to fiddle with it, but to no avail. It was busted. When I looked up again, I realized that Theo was gone. We'd been separated. I was just a few kilometres from the city. I could see lights in the distance, but without my GPS, I didn't know where to find the finish line.

I made my way towards the city and then wandered around for a while, wasting valuable time. A great wall surrounded the city. I ran along the side of the wall hoping to find a way in, but I didn't see anything, no gate or door. Finally, I found a small door. I knocked on it, and a man answered. I asked him how to get into the city, and he gave me directions. It was all done in a language somewhere between mime, French, and English.

I ran down the streets of Agadez, looking for the finish line. I eventually stumbled on it purely by chance. I saw Alain standing there, and next to him, Theo. Oh well. Third place it is, I thought. I didn't feel bad at all. I learned a lesson, but I was also very proud of my finish. There were amazing runners at the Trans 333.

When I returned home, I called up Charlie Engle, my buddy from the Jungle Marathon.

"Ever wonder whether anyone's ever run across the entire Sahara Desert?" I asked him.

"Hmm," he said.

"I mean, how big could it be? Thirty-five hundred kilometres?" I said.

Little did I know that not only was the Sahara far, far bigger than that, but I would be running across it several years later. I couldn't stop thinking about that little girl without any water. Something about running through the desert in Niger had planted the seed of an idea in my mind, but it hadn't yet blossomed. I had no idea what I was in for, but that's a long story, and maybe best saved for another time.

# CHAPTER EIGHTEEN

The Race of Failure
July 2005

After Trans 333, I started working with Lisa Smith-Batchen. We communicated online and over the phone. I had decided to enter The Badwater Ultramarathon, one of the toughest footraces in the world, but before that, I wanted to compete in the 20th annual Marathon des Sables. I had almost five months to prepare for it. I'd been racing regularly for almost a year, and although taking five months off seemed like a long time, I had good reason. First of all, getting to a race costs a lot of money, so I was going to have to work my butt off to save enough to get out to Morocco and then California. I wanted to do my best out there, and five months of training could only improve me. But, more important, there was also Kathy. I wanted to spend as much time with her as possible. I loved her, and being away from her all the time was tough. I wanted to ask her to marry me, but I was waiting for the perfect time.

Lisa e-mailed me a training program every couple of weeks. It was amazing to have a coach, especially because I'd never had one before. Knowing that someone believed in me as an athlete meant so much to me. I felt very lucky: I had a network of people that supported what I was doing, but now I had a coach too. Everything seemed in place.

Having a coach wasn't just about support though. As a personal trainer myself, I knew I'd be better off having someone else to work with. Attempting to plan your own fitness program doesn't always work. You think you know your own limits but a good coach, like Lisa, will help you see a fresh perspective and get you to the next level of performance.

Lisa sent me e-mails with specific workouts for ten or fourteen days at a time. Some days, she'd have me running up and down hills for hours. Sometimes she'd have me doing long runs day after day in an effort to prepare me for Marathon des Sables. The one constant was that every program she gave me was about making me a better runner. She had me running six days a week, something I'd never done before. In fact, I'd told myself that I couldn't. But when Lisa told me I could, I listened. The limits we set in our own minds aren't always reality, and having Lisa coach me reminded me of that.

I went back to Marathon des Sables in April of 2005, armed with everything I'd learned from the year before. It was a neat year to be there. The 20th anniversary had brought out some incredible runners, and the race organizers pulled out all the stops to make it a memorable year. Some say the 20th edition was one of the most competitive ever. They even organized a professional opera in the middle of the desert. I've never seen anything like that before. I did much better in 2005 than I had the year before. I was the first North American runner, came in 24th overall, and, most important, I improved my speed and came home feeling good about it.

After the Marathon des Sables, I went out to Lisa's Badwater Training Camp in Jackson Hole, Wyoming. Marshall Ulrich was going to be coaching, and I knew I had to meet him. Marshall was a true legend. Among a variety of awe-inspiring accomplishments, he'd completed over a hundred ultramarathons, had finished Badwater over a dozen times, and had climbed each of the Seven Summits! I wanted to learn everything and anything I could from him. Lisa invited me to come to the camp as an instructor, so I taught a seminar on core strength, but I also participated in the training activities.

The Badwater Ultra is a non-stop 135-mile (215K) footrace in California. It begins at the Badwater Basin in Death Valley, nearly three hundred feet below sea level, and ends at the Mount Whitney summit, which stands at nearly fifteen thousand feet, the highest point in the contiguous United States. That alone would make it an incredibly tough race, but it gets worse: the heat of Death Valley can climb up to 55°C!

I enjoyed the training camp that Lisa and Marshall staged and felt more prepared for the race afterwards. It was going to be a total departure for me because I'd never done a road race at that point. I'd raced all over the planet—in sand, in jungle, on ice— but I'd never raced on a plain old road. That was what had me so excited; it wasn't normally my thing, and I was looking forward to the challenge.

Badwater is a fully supported road race. You need a crew to man the vehicles that follow and support you during the run. The pavement is so hot that runners are constantly dousing themselves in ice. A runner usually has two vehicles: one to follow you and one to make trips to the nearest towns for necessities. I had no idea how I was going to organize that. Luckily, Marshall Ulrich recommended a friend of his to me. Teresa had crewed for other runners at Badwater, so she would definitely be an asset.

When I returned from the training camp, I asked Anton Stranc, a friend I had met at the Peak Centre, if he would head my team as crew chief. Anton is an incredibly accomplished tri-athlete, so I knew he'd understand what it would take to organize a challenge like Badwater. Anton agreed. He was amazing, and I knew I was lucky to have him.

My goal for Badwater was simple: I wanted to finish the

race. I wasn't concerned with placing. I wasn't doing it to run competitively. I figured I could always come back again another year and try for a better performance, but in 2005, all I wanted to do was finish.

Once I had Anton and Teresa on my team, I still had to recruit a few others. Lisa had a client in Toronto named Clay who was willing to help out, and Teresa enlisted one of her friends, a nurse named Joanne. By then, we had a team.

To prepare for the race, I ran on pavement as much as possible and did long runs through Gatineau Park. After the 2005 race at Marathon des Sables, several months of training, and Lisa's training camp in Wyoming, I felt pretty confident.

Anton and I flew to Las Vegas, where we picked up the van and then drove out of the city towards California. I wasn't sorry I didn't have a chance to see more of Vegas. Once we left the city, the peace of the desert began to take over. It was quiet and still. The drive into Death Valley took us about four hours. It was beautiful. We drove through magnificent mountains, and below us, I could see deep valleys.

We met the rest of the crew at the Furnace Creek Ranch. I was excited to meet them. Clay, Joanne, and Teresa were all amazing, and everyone had pockets of experience that would prove to be quite useful. The girls had already picked up our other vehicle, a car, and they got busy preparing signage for both the van and the car. Badwater has a lot of rules for the race, one of them being that support vehicles need to be properly identified as such, since they're driving on public roads. Ultimately, all the rules are there to protect racers and crew alike.

My crew didn't want me standing outside in the heat, so they shooed me away into the lodge. It was *amazingly* hot.

I'd been in deserts before, but this was something entirely different. It was the hottest place I'd ever been. Just the heat coming off the road alone was enough to make me feel woozy. I thought I was going to melt!

I took my crew's advice and spent the rest of the day relaxing indoors. That night, we attended a pre-race event and then went back to the hotel for a huge meal. The place was teeming with elite runners from all over the world. I was humbled to be in their presence. I felt prepared, but at the same time, I couldn't help being a little nervous. There were just so many good runners!

I awoke the next morning ready to race. My crew had everything prepared. I went down to the start line. Even in the early morning, it was incredibly hot. Above us there was a cliff with a line painted on it to show where sea level was. We were a few hundred feet below it! Next to the start line was a small pool of saltwater—Badwater is named after this pool, since the water in it is undrinkable.

There was lots of commotion before the race began. Pictures were being taken and everyone was excited. I saw Charlie, Lisa, Marshall, and Jack Denness, as well as a number of other famous runners, including Pam Reed and Ferg Hawke (who is Canadian and came in 2nd place that year!)

I was slightly overwhelmed to be grouped with these runners, but I reminded myself that I was feeling good and that running on the road couldn't be as tough as running with a heavy pack in the sand. Man oh man, was I ever wrong!

I stood at the bottom of Badwater Basin. My crew was a short ways ahead in the vehicles. I took several deep breaths. I was nervous, but I knew I could handle the race. The gun went off, and I started to run along the side of the highway.

I started the first leg of the journey, towards Furnace Creek

Ranch, at a pretty good clip. At every mile marker, my crew was right there, ready to hand me water and mist me down. Teresa, with her clipboard in hand, told me I was putting down a good time. I felt good too. It was hot—hotter than two deserts combined—but things seemed to be going well.

When I made it to the first checkpoint at Furnace Creek, 17 miles in, I still felt good. Anton was continually handing me water. I drank from the bottles he provided but often didn't finish them. I felt hydrated enough. I kept going. Stovepipe Wells was the next destination, a small outpost with a gas station, motel, and restaurant, somewhere around the 40-mile point.

Everything was working like a charm. As I plodded along, my support crew had everything under control. At every mile marker, all I had to do was slow down. Anton would hand me a bottle, while Joanne removed the earphones from my MP3 player and Clay placed an ice necklace around my neck. Teresa recorded what I ate, what I drank, and my average speed.

At one point, I started to slow.

"Ray, you're dipping below your average speed," Teresa informed me.

I couldn't seem to go any faster. I continued to slow down until I felt the need to walk.

"Here, drink this," Anton said as he tried to hand me some Gatorade, but I waved it away in a daze.

As I rounded a corner and headed towards the Devil's Corn Field (an apt name if ever there was one), the wind coming down the road was so hot I felt like I was standing in front of a blast furnace. I actually laughed: I couldn't believe *anything* could be so hot! This must be what hell is like, I thought.

I told myself I just needed to make it to Stovepipe Wells

and that everything would be all right once I got there, but it seemed to take an eternity. My crew hollered out encouragement, but it felt like I was running on the spot. As I would sweat, it would instantly evaporate. Anton kept trying to give me more water, more hydration fluid. I drank as much as I could. Still, I wasn't peeing at all. I knew I was probably a little dehydrated.

When I finally made it to the checkpoint at Stovepipe Wells, I was ecstatic to see they had set up a massage table. Teresa massaged my legs and I had something to eat, but before I knew it, my fifteen minutes were up and I had to get going again. It had gone by in a snap. The next checkpoint was just less than 20 miles away. Townes Pass, I told myself. Just make it to Townes Pass. I started to move.

I heard my name called and turned around to see Charlie.

"How's it going?" he asked.

"To be honest," I said, "I don't feel great. I feel sort of funny. Do you want to walk for a bit?"

Charlie was feeling good and wanted to press on.

"Okay," I said, "Maybe I'll catch up to you later."

I walked a couple of miles before I felt the urge to pee. I took that as a good sign: I couldn't remember the last time I'd gone.

I stopped and stood by the side of the road. When I looked down, I saw that my pee looked strange. It was as brown as Coke and as thick as syrup. I knew then that something was wrong. Oh shit, I thought. What's happening?

I alerted my crew. Joanne looked concerned.

"You must be really dehydrated," she said.

Just then, my legs started to cramp. I'd never felt anything like it. It was like my muscles were literally being torn from my legs. My lower body seized up completely. I couldn't even walk. I wanted to sit down, but the heat of the road would certainly burn me.

"I'll be okay," I said. "Just let me rest for one minute, and then I'll go...."

Even as I said it, I knew it wasn't true. The light of consciousness started to fade. The next thing I knew, I woke up in the medical tent, where a team of nurses were hovering above me.

"I'm okay," I said. "I have to get back on the course."

"You're not going anywhere until you drink those," one of them said, and pointed at several bottles of Gatorade.

I wasn't going to argue. I downed them. A doctor came by and warned me that he was concerned I had done damage to my kidneys. But when I peed again, it was a much better colour and I was allowed to leave the tent.

It was completely dark by the time we got back to the course. My crew was encouraging. I started to walk, hoping to build back up to a run, but my legs hurt tremendously. Still I tried. Every step was brutal. Several hours passed before I started to literally fall asleep on my feet. It was like I wasn't there. I was a zombie. I fell down on my knees. My feet weren't working, and neither were my legs. Worse, my mind wasn't with me anymore. It was over, and I knew it.

"That's it, buddy," Anton said.

I was finished. There was no way I was going to make it to Mount Whitney. There were tears in my eyes. My whole world felt like it was caving in. I got into the van and asked Anton to take me back to Stovepipe Wells so I could place a call to Kathy. I wanted to cry.

"I had to drop out," I told her.

Kathy knew how much every race meant to me. How much time and money, sweat and determination, had gone into my preparation.

"Did you try your best?" she asked. I knew it hurt her to hear how terrible I felt.

"Yes," I said sadly.

Maybe that was the problem, I thought. Maybe I'd tried my best and it still wasn't good enough. I had to fight back the tears again. Maybe I'd been fooling myself.

"Then there's nothing else you could have done," she said. "When your head clears, we'll figure out what went wrong."

When I put the phone down, I still wasn't thinking clearly. I liked the message that Kathy was giving me, but I wasn't convinced. We went back to the lodge. I fell into a deep sleep for hours. By the next morning, I was able to feel my legs again. We drove out to Mount Whitney to cheer the racers on.

When the race was over, I went to the awards ceremony. I went out of respect for the runners who had finished and because I wanted to clap for the Canadian racers. There weren't that many of us out there, so I wanted to show my support. I felt very emotional at the ceremony as I watched other Badwater first-timers go up to receive their finisher's medal. I didn't understand what I had done wrong. My friends attempted to console me. People kept reminding me that everyone has a bad race now and again, but I just wasn't absorbing it.

At one point during the ceremony, they called out the names of those of us who didn't finish. There were more than I'd expected: fourteen, including myself. When they called us out, I was the only one to stand up. Actually, I was the only one who had attended. So there were others who were feeling the same pain as me. I lightened up a bit. I was even able to laugh at myself. But I still didn't have a handle on what had gone wrong.

# CHAPTER NINETEEN

A Higher Elevation
July 2005

My failure to complete the race at Badwater weighed on me heavily. I thought about it all the way home, and no matter what I told myself, I still felt terrible. I'd spent a fortune to get there, brought a crew of people out to help, and worked hard for months. It wasn't just that. The idea that maybe I'd simply lost my ability—that it had just disappeared—tormented me.

Once home, I had a strange antsy feeling. After so many years of hard work, after changing my thinking habits to become more positive, I slipped into an older version of myself. I wondered whether I was throwing my life away. I knew that I was doing what I loved, and I knew that was important, but I also started to question whether I was doing the right thing. I considered the possibility that maybe I should stop spending all my time and money chasing a dream I'd never be able to catch.

I took all these fears to my parents. I knew that when I had first started to run, they weren't sure whether to take it seriously. After failing at Badwater, they could have tried to talk me out of racing entirely. But that wasn't what happened at all. In fact, when I returned from Death Valley, I learned that my parents had actually been following all of my exploits. They were so proud of me that they made a point of keeping other family members abreast of where I was and what I was doing.

They understood that running was the path I had chosen. Neither of them could really grasp why I'd want to do something as obscene as run through desert climates for hundred of kilometres at a time, but they appreciated my desire and my fortitude. They were truly proud of me!

It meant so much to me to know that they supported what I was doing with my life. Since my dad's stroke, he'd become a man of few words. It was a difficult thing to adjust to, especially because he'd been such a buoyant exuberant character. After listening to my story about the race, my father looked at me and said something I really needed to hear.

"Don't give up," he said.

And he meant it.

"If there's one thing I know about you, it's that you have the ability to learn from your mistakes. Be rational about this, and try again."

His words began a healing process. Later that day, I talked to Lisa.

"How much were you drinking exactly?" she asked matter-of-factly.

I looked at my charts. Son of a bitch! I don't know why I hadn't seen it sooner. Suddenly, everything was incredibly obvious. I hadn't drank *nearly* enough. I don't know why. I'd felt okay, so I'd taken my hydration for granted. Big mistake. But at least I knew what my mistake had been!

"You didn't drink enough," Lisa told me. "You didn't get enough fluid in you. You were probably dehydrated within the first fifteen miles. You can't recover after that! You screwed up, buddy. I hope you learn something from it."

If Lisa's words sound harsh, it's only because you have to know Lisa to know what a tough, caring, and kick-ass coach she really is. I remembered how dehydrated I had become in the Yukon, how it had gotten so bad out there that I'd begun to hallucinate. I thought about Marathon des Sables and the Jungle Marathon, where I'd made a whole-hearted effort not to let that happen again. Why had I slipped up at Badwater? I had taken it for granted. It was a wake-up call.

I knew I had to stop beating myself up over what happened at Badwater. The whole notion of failure was just part of the old me trying to creep back in. I didn't want to be someone who gave up when the going got tough. I knew that if I just stopped—stopped doing the thing I loved and was passionate about—that would be the true failure. Staying properly hydrated had been my first challenge at my first race. There was no way I'd let it be the end of my career too!

A few days later, I talked to Charlie. He'd done really well at Badwater and placed 3$^{rd}$. I was happy for him.

"I don't know what to do next," I told Charlie. Even though I knew why things had gone wrong, I was still apprehensive about how to proceed.

"There's a race in the desert," Charlie told me. "It's in Egypt. Kevin's going. It's a Racing the Planet event, and it's going to be in the Sahara. Why don't you just go for it? Retrain for something fresh?"

It sounded like a good idea. I wanted to redeem myself. For my own sake, I wanted to prove to myself that I could do it.

"Listen," Charlie said. "Shit happens, buddy. You'll conquer Badwater another time. In the meantime, do the Sahara race."

I knew he was right.

"And you know what else?" Charlie said, sounding excited. "You know this idea about running across the entire Sahara?"

"Yeah...." I said. Of course I remembered. It was a dream. I'd thought about constantly since coming back from Niger.

"Well, it might just be a reality." Charlie said.

"What? Really?" I asked. I couldn't believe it.

"Don't get too excited yet. I'll keep you posted," he said. "Oh, and by the way, the Sahara's a lot bigger than you thought."

That was all he could tell me. I tried not to get too excited. Instead, I channelled my energy into this new race. It was part of something called The 4 Deserts series, and each race would take place in a different desert in a different part of the world. The one in Egypt would be the inaugural Sahara event.

If I could get some of the race sponsored, and if I worked my ass off all summer, I could afford to go. If I ate right, trained right, and stayed focused, I could combat my doubt with seeds of hope. I needed to show myself that I could do it.

All throughout the summer, I kept a stiff upper lip. A part of me was terrified that I wouldn't be able to handle the race. On the other hand, I had so much support from friends and family, and I knew that I was doing the right thing for me. I committed to the race, to the lifestyle, and I trained hard. When I caught myself having a negative thought, I made a conscious effort to fight it with a positive one. You'd be surprised how well that works if you really give it a fair shake.

Even Kathy got in on the action. She had started running longer distances by then and would often go out on trail runs with me. Having her there helped us bond. I knew that she was beginning to understand why I loved to do what I did. I felt as though we were more involved, both spiritually and emotionally, than we had ever been. We were truly sharing our lives. I knew it was time to propose.

I thought about it long and hard. I wanted to celebrate how I felt in a unique way. I had visions of hiring a hot-air balloon and painting it with the words "Will you marry me?" I thought about hiring a plane and popping the question ten thousand feet up in the air. I came up with a hundred corny ideas. What I was searching for was something that would be truly meaningful to Kathy. I didn't think she'd want anything flashy; it just isn't her style. I wanted it to be something we'd remember for the rest of our lives. I thought about the first time we went hiking. It had been on the Skyline trail, way up in Gatineau Park. It had been such a wonderful day.

I called Pat.

"I'm going to ask Kathy to marry me," I told him. "And I need your help."

Pat owned a restaurant and bar. I told him to put aside a bottle of champagne, glasses, a silver tray, and his tuxedo. We worked it all out.

A few weeks later, Kathy and I went to the core strength class I taught. She usually participated in the class and often helped out. The class was only forty-five minutes long but that day it seemed to go forever. I was going to ask her to marry me, and I was incredibly nervous. After class, I asked her if she felt like taking a hike.

"A hike?" She said, surprised. "You haven't asked me to go on a hike for so long!"

"Well, do you feel like it?" I asked.

"Sure!"

We drove out to the trail, parked the car, and started our hike up the tree-covered trail. The sun was beginning to set.

"Hey, we better make a lot of noise in case there are bears around," I said loudly.

"What are you talking about?" Kathy said. She laughed, thinking I was just being silly.

"We wouldn't want to startle them!" I said, almost yelling.

Of course I wasn't trying to ward off any bears. I was trying to make a lot of noise so that Pat would hear us coming. He was up on the trail in a tux with the ring in his pocket, and a bottle of champagne on a silver tray.

He heard me all right, and came barrelling down the trail dressed to the nines. Kathy was startled.

"Pat, what are you doing out here? What's with the suit? And the champagne?" she asked.

I just smiled. Pat set the tray down.

"I'll see you guys later," he said, and took off down the trail.

We were on a lookout. You could see Ottawa in the distance. I got down on one knee. Kathy looked shocked.

"Kathy, will you marry me?" I asked.

She didn't even have to think about it.

"Yes!" she said. "Yes!"

My heart felt as big as a hot-air balloon.

# CHAPTER TWENTY

The Race of Redemption
September 2005

In the week leading up to the Sahara race, I took care of every single detail I could think of. I weighed and re-weighed my pack. I cut off every exposed thread, every wayward tag. I couldn't have been more prepared. I had the right shoes, the right shorts. I was willing to skimp on my gear, but I refused to go light on my food. Not after the chicken gumbo fiasco. My main concern at that point was my entry fee. My gear and food had cost a bundle. I'd already paid off most of my entry fee, but not all of it. I was panic-stricken until Mike Edelson swooped in and saved the day, again.

The race was going to be 250K over a series of six days, so it was similar to the Marathon des Sables, but the rumour was that it would be more intense, since Ian Adamson had designed the course. He was known for extremely tough courses.

I flew from Montreal to Frankfurt, and then to Cairo. As I flew over Cairo, I looked down and saw what looked like a haze of dust over the city. There seemed to be a lot of action below. There were a lot of buildings, and I could make out the Nile too. I got the jitters. My stomach did a few back flips. I reminded myself that all I could do was my best. I promised myself I'd give it that much.

With my luggage in my hands, I left the airport, ready to go to the hotel. As soon as the doors opened, I smelled that smell again. It was so much like Morocco. I immediately felt cleansed of all my nervous energy. I don't know what it is

A sunrise over the Sahara

about that African desert smell, but it calms my nerves in a way that nothing else can.

When I walked into the hotel, I saw Kevin. I was so happy to see him! I had honestly come to think of him as a brother. We started to catch up, although both of us were nearly delirious from lack of sleep. Marshall Ulrich was there too, and tons of other runners started filing into the lobby. Before I knew it, there was a huge cast of characters milling about. Everyone was talking about what great runners had showed up. A Russian runner who had won the Gobi March the year before was there, and an amazing Olympic cross-country-skier-turned-ultramarathoner named Joe Holland had shown up. There was a British racer named Gary Johnson who looked incredibly strong. But my bet was on Kevin, who had already won a Racing the Planet event

Me and Kevin Lin at a checkpoint during the Sahara race

and was capable of a sub-2:20 marathon.

The competition was stiff, but fortunately for me, all I hoped to do was finish. As long as I did my best, I knew I'd be happy with that.

We did gear check the next day. There were over a hundred runners participating from all over the world. I thought that was really cool. One of the rules of the race was that every runner had to wear a flag of their country on their sleeve. I loved that. I felt so proud to have that maple leaf on my sleeve.

We headed out into the desert the next morning. I changed into my race clothes in the hotel and then got onto the bus. We spent the entire day riding west, deeper into the desert. I slept for long stretches of road. Occasionally, the bus would be forced to stop for military checkpoints. It was so strange to be confronted by dudes with guns on the side of the road, but we didn't have any problems and were allowed to move forward.

By the time we got to camp, it was dark. There was a big campfire set up, and the race organizers had prepared a meal. We all sat around the campfire, hanging out and sharing stories about past races. I noticed several competitors who looked incredibly tough, especially the Russian. I knew he was going kick some butt.

I thought about what Charlie had told me before I'd left for Egypt.

"When you start the race," he'd said, "watch the people around you. Run behind everyone. Don't take off fast. Just watch them. And then whatever happens, happens."

I remembered what Lisa had said too.

"Watch the way the others run, and see who's working harder than the others. You're trained for this, Ray," she'd said. "You're ready. I want you to know that."

On the start line the next morning, I was still thinking about what Lisa and Charlie had told me, but I wished they could see the other runners. They *all* looked serious. Kevin and I hugged and wished each other luck. I looked out at the desert. The floor was covered in a white substance that looked almost like snow. The gun went off.

We all started running down a rocky area. I could hear the sound of people's breathing getting heavier, so I turned up the tunes on my MP3 player. I didn't want to hear my breath or the sound of my feet hitting the ground. As we moved along we got into a sandier area. The Russian, who had been up in front, began to drop behind. He was an amazing runner, but I think the sand was getting to him. One by one, runners started to drop off. Before long, Kevin and I were alone. He got in behind my shoulder. The first stage was only 32K. It was hot. We kept running. At the first checkpoint, we grabbed our water and moved on. We came to the second checkpoint 10K later. We only had another 10K to go before the end of the first stage. I was feeling great.

"Kev, I feel really good," I told him. "I think I'm going to open it up and run a little harder."

I cranked my tunes and went forward. I thought Kevin was right behind me. When I ran through the first finish line, in 1$^{st}$ place, Ian Adamson was there, but the banners hadn't been put up yet.

"Wow," he said. "You ran that stage really fast."

I guess I had, though I hadn't really noticed. I'd been having so much fun that the time just flew by. Kevin came in a few minutes later. CNN was out there and I was interviewed. I couldn't believe they were covering the race.

Later that night, I heard a commotion coming from Kevin's tent. I ran in to see what it was all about, and there, on the side of the tent, was one of the nastiest spiders in existence. It looked like a hairless albino tarantula, and when one of the Egyptian runners tried to whack it with a shoe, it actually went *after* him, crawling at lightspeed. The thing moved as fast as a cockroach—faster, even—and my heart was beating even faster. They'd told us to be on the look out for vipers, but for the rest of the race, I slept with one eye open, hoping I didn't see another camel spider but wanting to be prepared if I did.

I woke up on the morning of the second day feeling groggy after a bad night's sleep. That giant spider had really disturbed me. I made some oatmeal and then lined up at the start line next to Kevin.

"We should run together," Kevin said.

The course was about 42K that day. We ran through

white rock and darker sand, and then back into the flaky stuff that looked like snow. Before long, Kevin and I were all alone again. Like the day before, I sped up towards the end of the stage and came in 1$^{st}$ place, with Kevin behind me in a close second. I couldn't believe I had won the first two stages. I didn't feel like I deserved to be ahead of Kevin.

It was so hot out there that cooking was a non-issue. You could literally cook your dehydrated foods by pouring drinking water on it and waiting for a minute or two. This was fine, if you wanted to cook, but it didn't do much for drinking water. Rumour had it that caps were exploding off of water bottles at some of the checkpoints. What I wouldn't have done for some ice! The water was so hot that it was unsatisfying. Someone came up with a great if slightly disgusting way to cool down your water. We wet a sock and wrapped it around the water bottle. As the water evaporated from the sock, it would cool the water down and made it bearable—if not enjoyable—to drink.

The third day and fourth day were 32K and 40K respectively. Kevin and I ran together. On both days, Gary Johnson, the British runner, beat us to the first checkpoint, but each time Kevin and I would overtake him by the end of the stage and come in 1$^{st}$ and 2$^{nd}$. Day four was interesting because we transitioned through several types of terrain. We went from the White Desert to the Black Desert, and then into more typical desert terrain. But as we got closer to the end of the stage, the course got more rocky and hilly and mountainous.

Everyone was a little apprehensive about the long day five. It was 80K, and it was the most critical day in a competitive sense. The final stage was only 10K, so day five was crucial. If you had a mind to place, you'd have to run the 80K fast, but you'd have to pace yourself too.

Taking a breather after a tough stage - Gobi March

That night, I read the course description of the fifth leg and tried to visually run through it in my mind. I pictured myself out there, giving it my all. I felt so good, and so lucky, that I was doing well. It's hard to describe the feeling. I'd come into the race feeling so low and unsure of myself. Winning the first four stages was doing wonders for my self-confidence. I felt satisfied. I wanted to do well on the long day but I ultimately didn't care about the general rankings anymore. I figured I'd already done well for myself, and I knew I'd be happy no matter how things turned out.

The next day, Kevin and I decided to run together. His strategy was to go out real easy for the first half and then run

Libyan Challenge

really hard in the second half. I was all for it.

"When we get to the second half," he said, "run at your own pace. But let's run the first half easy. If people want to run with us, fine. We keep a modest pace."

It seemed like a good strategy to me too.

Off we went. We began at 7 a.m., as part of the later wave of runners. The pack spread out pretty quickly. We ran with Joe Holland and Gary. Gary overtook us all and beat us to the first checkpoint, but he got tired after that and fell

Libyan Challenge

behind. Kevin and I kept a steady pace just as we had agreed.

Somewhere around the 35K mark, the desert became less sandy and rockier. Joe, Kevin, and I kept running together. We came over a ridge that dropped into a huge valley. When we got to the bottom Kevin gave me a hand signal. I knew what it meant. He wanted to test Joe out. He accelerated towards the 41K checkpoint. Kevin put the hammer down! I had a hard time keeping up, but Kevin insisted I stick it out. He wanted to see about Joe, to see if he could handle it. He could! Joe was awesome: a force to be reckoned with!

The halfway point was a mandatory stop. We took off our shoes and relaxed for a bit. We had as much food and water as we could stomach and then we prepared to leave.

The next checkpoint wasn't very far away. There was a tank of water there, big enough for the racers to swim in, but when we got there, neither Kevin nor I wanted to stop and get wet. Joe did. He jumped in the water and swam around to cool off. From there we ran through a small village. This had to be one of the highlights of the day for me. The villagers all waved at us as we rolled through, and some of the children ran behind us a ways. Their faces were all so sweet and smiling. I thought about the little girl in Niger who had made such an impression on me.

We left the village and went out into another rocky area that soon became almost mountainous terrain. My legs were starting to get tired, but I wanted to keep moving, so I told Kevin that I was going to accelerate my pace. I went up and down one hill after another. My legs became increasingly sore and my quads started to cramp. I wanted to stop and scream from the pain, but I wanted to get to the finish even more, so I pushed forward.

Just 7K from the finish, I saw a massive dune ahead of me. It was so big that I had to scramble up to the top, but when I did, I could see the finish line.

I'd gotten to know the Egyptian crewmembers over the course of the race. They had taken to calling me "Camel" and "Canada" and thought it was hilarious that this guy from the land of snow and ice was loving the desert. They were all singing and banging on drums at the finish line, and as I came in, they welcomed me with shouts and hollers. They clapped and sang, and I knew that they were sort of laughing at me and with me at the same time. I loved it!

After crossing the finish line, I realized that I had pretty much secured the win. It felt great to be first. It was my first solo victory since the Yukon. Kevin had laid the boots down in the last 8K, followed by Joe in 3rd place. The three of us were in incredibly high spirits and stayed up talking and joking around until we couldn't hold out any longer and crashed. Since the racers had thirty-six hours to complete the stage, runners were still coming in when I woke up the next morning. When everyone had made it in, we learned that we would actually be doing the final 10K in the streets of Cairo—the race would end at the base of the Sphinx. Everyone was incredibly excited.

Late that night, we climbed into Land Cruisers, and when we got to the road, we piled into buses and drove all night to get to Cairo. I woke up to find that we were stopped at the side of the road behind a main street. The bustle and energy of the city was insane. The poverty, too, was evident. There were streams of water clogged with garbage trickling through the streets, and buildings that looked dusty and neglected. On the other hand, there were also old buildings that looked beautiful and well maintained.

When the last leg of this amazing race began, I started off on the road next to Kevin but I couldn't keep up with him—road races being his speciality. As I ran towards the finish line I wrapped around the back end of the pyramids. As I approached the Sphinx, I saw Gary. I stopped and waited for him to approach. We were 500 metres from the Sphinx and at the top of a small hill.

"Let's go down this hill together," I said.

We grabbed hands and ran. Just before we got to the finish line, a Canadian athlete named Wade Bloomer, who had been injured during the race, handed me the Canadian flag.

I had Gary's hand in mine, and in the other, I held the flag of my country. I had never been so proud to hold that flag as I was then, running across that finish line towards a victory that I hadn't asked for but badly needed. Everyone was there. Kevin stood proudly with his flag of Taiwan. It felt so good to finish in 1$^{st}$ and 2$^{nd}$ place with him. It made an incredible experience that much better.

It was a wonderful feeling. All the mistakes, the hard work, the blood, sweat, and tears, had paid off. I looked behind me at the Sphinx and the pyramids. I couldn't believe I was really there, in front of one of the Seven Wonders of the World. I felt like the Sahara Race was one of the wonders of my own life.

I completed two more races before Kathy and I were married in the summer of 2006. Both went incredibly well. I placed 1$^{st}$ at the Libyan Challenge in February 2006, a 190K non-stop race. It took me roughly thirty-one hours. Then in May, Charlie, Kevin and I won as a team at the Gobi March in China.

# Chapter Twenty One

The Ultimate Victory
August 2006

As soon as I got home from the Gobi Desert in China, Kathy and I went into full swing preparing for the wedding. There were so many people we wanted to invite, but hosting a wedding of that size was going to break the bank. It just wasn't possible.

Greg Christie had been to Tanzania the year before on vacation. We heard all about the trip and how wonderful it had been. He'd hired guides through a locally owned touring company. Kathy and I thought it might be a good honeymoon destination, but we figured we probably couldn't afford it. But when Greg told us how much it had cost, we reconsidered. It wasn't outrageous. I looked at Kathy. I could tell she had an idea.

"Ray?" she asked me. "Why don't we just go to Africa and get married there?"

It was an awesome idea! I was elated. Us! Together! In Tanzania! I'd never been to sub-Saharan Africa, and I loved the idea that we'd be going somewhere that was totally new for both of us.

Greg gave us the names and telephone numbers of his guides. We telephoned The Black Mamba Travel Co. in Arusha and spoke with Leonard and Lilly, the guides that Greg had so highly recommended. Everything was doable. The only problem was breaking the news to our family.

At first, everyone felt a bit jilted. But what about the wedding?! That was a common refrain in the beginning. After all, we were essentially eloping. It took a little bit of

The last camp before heading to the summit of Kilimanjaro

time, but eventually our parents reluctantly admitted that our plan did seem in keeping with our lifestyle and would save us a lot of money. We assured them that as soon as we came home, we'd have a big party in Harbour Grace: a backyard reception party with barbeque and beer, moose sausage and salmon, and, most important, our family and friends. Everyone was satisfied. Besides, they knew we were going to do it anyway.

We planned a ten-day trip in Tanzania. In those ten days, we'd have a look around the city, get married, and then for our honeymoon, we'd climb Mount Kilimanjaro. Our guides would organize everything, including the priest and the wedding site, which was, they said, a surprise. Everything was set. Kathy's sister Heather and brother-in-law Mick took

Enjoying the view on Kilimanjaro

us to the airport, where they pulled out their video camera and documented our last days as boyfriend and girlfriend.

We flew to Amsterdam, but when we got there, we found that our flight to Kilimanjaro International Airport had been overbooked. There were no seats for us on the plane.

"But we're getting married!" Kathy said to the young woman who worked for the airline.

The woman seemed sympathetic.

"Married?" she said. "Let me see what I can do."

And just like that, as if by magic, we were back on our way to Tanzania. I was so excited to be going to Africa again, and this time with Kathy and for the most important day of our lives.

Our guide Lilly greeted us at the airport. She was very

friendly and warm. As we walked over to her car, I noticed that the air smelled different than it did in Morocco. It was still sweet, but something about it was different. I liked that. I wanted every part of our experience to be unique—something special and new for both of us.

Lilly didn't know much English, but we managed to communicate very well regardless. She told us that she was glad to have us with her, that she had found us a lovely place to stay, and that she and Leonard were planning our wedding.

It was dark by the time we got to our lodge on the outskirts of town. We had our own little cabin. There was a slight scent of salt breeze in the air, and the cabin was surrounded by a plethora of flowers and foliage. Even in the dark, I could tell that it was utterly beautiful and lush.

"Wait until morning," the manager of the lodge told us. "Tomorrow, you will see Mount Meru and Kilimanjaro in the distance."

The next day, Lilly and Leonard came to pick us up. They drove us around the city and provided some insight into the local culture. We stopped at a thriving local market and ate nyama choma, a kind of Tanzanian roast meat, which was delicious. The local architecture reminded me of the villages I had seen in Brazil—simple structures with thatched roofs, but there were also many modern looking buildings as well. The four of us walked around the central district and I noticed that the city seemed to host many different cultures. Lilly told us that there were something like eighty tribes in Tanzania, and that they were all able to live together harmoniously. I thought that spoke volumes about the country. In the distance, I could see Mount Kilimanjaro, snow-capped and majestic, looming over the savannah.

The village children on our wedding day

On the day we were to be married, Kathy and I stood in front of our lodge and admired the view. Through a light fog, we could see the earthy tones of Mount Meru in the distance. Kathy looked beautiful in her dress. I had the rings in my pocket.

Lilly and Leonard showed up with a small entourage and two vehicles. Lilly presented Kathy with a gift: a traditional Tanzanian scarf. It was blue and very pretty, and Kathy placed it around her shoulders like a shawl.

"Okay," Leonard told us. "It's our tradition. You can't ride in the same vehicle as your fiancée. You," he said, looking at me, "have to ride with me. Kathy will go with Lilly."

We got into the cars, but we still didn't know where we were going. We cut through Arusha and got onto a trail road. Then we began to drive up towards the mountain. We drove for about an hour and a half, and then stopped in a small agricultural village at the base of Mount Meru. It seemed to me the perfect place. We met the priest who would perform our ceremony. All the kids in the village gathered round; Kathy played with them. For the first time in my life, I could imagine being a father.

The ceremony was short and sweet. Leonard and Lilly acted as our witnesses. As soon as the priest pronounced us man and wife, Leonard stepped in.

"Wait! Wait!" he said. "It's not over yet!"

Leonard ran to the car and emerged with a large cake that Lilly had bought. He brought out a bottle of wine, and we all shared it. As Lilly began to cut the cake into slices, Kathy stopped her.

"We have to make sure there's enough for all the kids!"

Lilly cut the cake into as many tiny pieces as she could. There were nearly forty little kids! They grabbed their pieces and ran away to eat them, then tried to sneak back in line to get a second piece—but they couldn't fool us! Their little faces were covered in icing! We wanted to make sure everyone got a taste.

As Leonard tried to control the kids, with Kathy laughing and playing with them, I stared off at Mount Meru. It seemed like such a perfect place to be on our wedding day. I knew that Kathy and I would have many mountains to climb, but I also knew that like the mountain, our love would be impossible to move.

I thought back to the day I climbed my first mountain with John. I had told myself that I always wanted my life to be full of passion and wonder. Now it was. I had come so

Me and Kathy on our wedding day

far, and I was so happy, but I knew that this moment was the beginning of a new life, one in which there would be many amazing things to look forward to. The possibilities for happiness were endless. The vision of the future looked wonderful, and Kathy would be there every step of the way. Tomorrow we would climb Mount Kilimanjaro. But I didn't want to focus on that just yet. I just wanted to be where I was.

# Index

Made in the USA
Lexington, KY
09 June 2014